Praise

"*Tried and True* tackles what most marriage resources miss: the spiritual disconnection at the root of so many relationship struggles. Dana Che masterfully weaves together the raw, real stories of twelve biblical couples, from Adam and Eve to Priscilla and Aquila, giving you both timeless wisdom and practical tools to deepen your connection with God and each other. This isn't just another marriage book; it's a journey for couples, with conversation starters, reflection questions, and guided prayers designed to spark open, honest, and transparent communication that creates extraordinary marriages. If you've been longing to experience true spiritual intimacy with your spouse, this book will meet you right where you are."

—Tony and Alisa DiLorenzo
Best-selling authors of *The 6 Pillars of Intimacy*® and hosts of the top-rated *One Extraordinary Marriage Podcast*
oneextraordinarymarriage.com

"*Tried and True* is not a comfort zone marriage book for couples—it's a transformational decision that leads you into the deep end of your marriage, inviting you to do the necessary and beautiful work of building intimacy through vulnerability, prayer, and meaningful conversations. Pastor Dana draws on biblical couples and her own hard-won expertise to guide you toward deeper understanding, intimacy, and faith.

This book does such a beautiful job of exploring biblical folks and applying their lessons to our lives. It's also rooted in Jesus and points couples to Him continually throughout the book as the main source of wellness and strength. And then! As if that's not enough, Pastor Dana invites you to explore your marriage through a coaching lens. Commit to these twelve chapters, and you will find, as I have, that your marriage has a new spring in its step, that you feel closer to God and deeply connected to your spouse."

—Nicole Langman
Therapist, Speaker, and Author of
You Are Wanted–Reclaiming the Truth of Who You Are
nicolelangman.com

"*Tried and True* is a hope-filled marriage resource that reminds couples they're not alone in their struggles and that God has always been faithful in the lives of marriages just like ours. Dana Che beautifully weaves together Scripture, relatable marriage challenges, and practical wisdom that draws couples closer to God and to one another. This book offers real solutions rooted in biblical truth. An encouraging resource for any couple wanting a stronger, more faith-filled marriage."

—Chris and Jamie Bailey
Christian Marriage Counselors and Founders of Expedition Marriage
expeditionmarriage.org

"In a moment when words written and spoken are cheap and overly abundant, *Tried and True* provides profound truth around identity and relationships. By providing fresh insight to familiar scriptural texts, Pastor Dana leads the reader down a wonderful mix of information and points of reflection. A must-read for every believer looking to grow in their walk with God or walk with others."

—Joel Solomon
Lead Pastor, New Life Church, Virginia Beach, VA
newlife.global

"*Tried and True* profiles twelve biblical couples, highlighting their unique challenges and life lessons. Through insights gained from these biblical relationships, along with Pastor Dana's candid sharing of the trials and tests in her own marriage, practical and life-changing truths are unlocked from the Word of God. As you read this devotional with an open heart and mind, you, your spouse, and your marriage will be profoundly changed."

—Kevin H. Turpin
Senior Associate Pastor, New Life Church, Virginia Beach, VA
President and Founder, Life Enrichment Center
lecliteracy.org

"*Tried and True* is a powerful book for couples, and Dana's transparency about her own marriage struggles drew me in immediately—it felt like sitting down with a trusted friend. I love how she anchors every insight in Scripture, drawing wisdom from real marriages in the Bible. This book doesn't shy away from tough, real-life topics that couples face every day, so if you're ready to deal with real and hard relationship issues, buckle up! If you're looking for something authentic, biblical, and deeply encouraging for your marriage, this is it."

—Vicki Gray
Co-Founder and Chief of Staff, Transformation Church, transformationchurch.tc

"Tried and True is a unique marriage book addressing a wide array of topics relevant to couples today. Pastor Dana gently guides couples through hard subjects with care, scriptural insight, and even humor with her unique brand of coaching. I wholeheartedly recommend this book to engaged couples seeking to strengthen their preparation, and for couples in all seasons of marriage who desire to maintain vitality and connection."

—Dorena Williamson
Author, Bridge-builder, and Associate Pastor of Belonging, Strong Tower Bible Church
dorenawilliamson.com

FOR MARRIAGES IN THE MIDDLE

TRIED
and TRUE

Marriage Advice from
12 Imperfect Biblical Couples

DANA CHE

CHESED
PRESS

Cover design: Usama Zaheen
Published by Chesed Press
ISBN 979-8-9940840-0-7 (paperback)
ISBN 979-8-9940840-1-4 (e-book)
ISBN 979-8-9940840-2-1 (audiobook)

DEDICATION

I dedicate this book to my husband, Shaun, my lover and friend. Our marriage has been through the kiln as fire tests gold. I remain grateful for your willing heart, unending support, and courageous resilience.

We, my love, are becoming tried and true.

These trials will show that your faith is genuine. It is being tested as fire tests and purifies gold—though your faith is far more precious than mere gold. So when your faith remains strong through many trials, it will bring you much praise and glory and honor on the day when Jesus Christ is revealed to the whole world.

1 Peter 1:7

Contents

Introduction

Marriage usually doesn't fall apart in a single moment of crisis. More often, it wears thin in the long middle—where expectations collide with reality, prayers go unanswered, and connection slowly gives way to routine. This is where many couples find themselves ... still committed, still believing, yet quietly wondering why connection feels harder than it used to.

I wrote this book to fill that gap. A significant part of my work is helping couples to strengthen intimacy on every level—emotional, physical, intellectual, recreational, and especially spiritual. Throughout our nearly thirty years of marriage, my husband Shaun and I have learned that intimacy doesn't sustain itself; it must be intentionally cultivated. True intimacy deepens our love for both God and each other.

Tried and True offers a way forward for couples who aren't looking for quick fixes but for a deeper, lasting connection that can withstand time and pressure. This book is the one I needed. My marriage has been through the fire. I kept trying to fix it, but I didn't realize I was starting from the wrong side. It's like trying to soothe a toothache by brushing your teeth. You've got to go deeper than that.

After working with so many couples in crisis, I've learned that *spiritual disconnection* is one of the most common—and least recognized—roots of marital breakdown.

I named this book *Tried and True* because the biblical marriages we'll study—both the triumphs and the trials—have faithfully stood the test of time in scripture. Pain, temptation, misunderstandings, and sometimes outright betrayal tried these couples. Yet through it all, God's goodness, love, and faithfulness proved true. Their stories will help you discover a deeper spiritual connection with God and with your spouse.

Let's be honest: most of our conversations with our spouses revolve around schedules, kids, money, and everyday responsibilities. What we rarely make time for is discussing God's Word or praying together. Yet those are the very moments where our deepest connection is formed. God's Word is what infuses our marriage with wisdom, healing, and hope.

But if you're new to the Christian faith or struggle in your relationship with God, reading the Bible can feel challenging. That's why I've included these biblical stories. Every time Jesus taught publicly, He used a story (Mark 4:34), because stories help truth take root in our hearts.

This book is multifaceted. It is designed as part self-help, part Bible study, part devotional, and part spiritual intimacy practice. Each section provides insight into a different biblical couple—including well-known stories such as Adam and Eve, Abraham and Sarah, and Mary and Joseph—while also highlighting lesser-known stories, such as Jacob and Leah, Deborah and Lappidoth, David and Michal, and Abigail and Nabal.

You'll see the good, the bad, and the ugly sides of their relationships. Some of their stories will move you to cheer; some will move you to tears. But in every single one, you'll catch glimpses of God's heart for marriage and His desire to be at the center of your love story.

I've been praying for you—that God will speak directly to you through the pages of this book. I can't wait for you to dive in.

HOW TO USE THIS BOOK

BIBLICAL INSIGHT: Each chapter explores the lives of twelve biblical couples and the lessons God's Word teaches through their flaws. Read at your own pace, and let these insights inspire, challenge, and remind you of God's faithfulness in your marriage.

PRACTICAL APPLICATION: Apply these meaningful but straightforward habits to put what you've learned into practice in your own relationship.

CONVERSATION STARTERS AND REFLECTION QUESTIONS: Use these tools to foster open, honest communication with your spouse, invite God into your conversations, and nurture your spiritual intimacy. Use the conversation starters on date nights or while driving. Your conversations don't have to be long or formal; they just need to be honest and open.

PRAYER REQUESTS: At the end of each chapter, you'll also find a space to write down your prayer requests and pray for them together. What are you believing God for right now?

GUIDED PRAYERS: The prayers provided at the end of each chapter are meant to serve as a springboard to get you started, but the real power comes when you make them your own, inviting God into the specific joys and struggles of your marriage.

Make it your goal not only to learn about these couples but also to begin seeing your own marriage in a new light. What does it mean to cover each other as Joseph did for Mary? To serve side by side like Priscilla and Aquila? To work through feelings of rejection like Leah? To face down betrayal like Hosea? These aren't just ancient stories; they are timeless truths that can transform the way you love each other today.

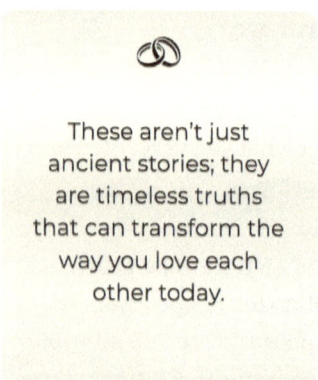

These aren't just ancient stories; they are timeless truths that can transform the way you love each other today.

So, grab your spouse, open your hearts, and invite God into this journey. Let these stories spark unforgettable conversations, stir up forgiveness and grace, and rekindle a greater sense of purpose and passion in your marriage.

Tried and True is an invitation to greater spiritual intimacy. I believe this is a God-opportunity for you and your spouse to grow together as you experience God's purpose for an enduring covenant.

A word to *solo spouses*: If you're turning these pages without your spouse—whether they're unable or unwilling right now, take heart. Your courage to seek growth on your own is a powerful first step toward change.

Are you ready? Let's step into the stories of these ancient couples and discover how their lives can breathe a fresh fire into yours.

PART 1

Belief and Boundaries

1

Adam and Eve:
Naked and Unashamed

Finding God's Grace in Your Exposed Places

Now the man and his wife were both naked,
but they felt no shame.

Genesis 2:25

What image comes to mind when you see yourself naked?
Do you like what you see?

For me, it depends on my latest lifestyle choices. If
I've been *giving myself grace,* devouring too many chips and
guac, it's no bueno. If, however, I've been on track, killin'
the game, exercising alongside my favorite YouTube
fitness trainers and choosing organic raspberries over the
Sour Patch Kids that constantly call my name, it's a *heck
yeah!*

To be naked is to experience vulnerability in its
purest form—uncovered, unguarded, and fully seen

Before the Kardashian culture, most people refrained from running around the streets showing off their tushies and ... need I say more?

And as you've likely discovered, being naked in front of your spouse kind of comes with the marriage territory. Not only because nakedness precedes sex, but also because it precedes trust.

Nakedness was God's original idea.

Follow me into the Garden of Eden.

After God created the sun, moon, and stars, as well as the lions, tigers, and bears (*oh my*), He created man and woman. He gave most animals fur, but to the man and woman, He gave only fine, little hairs that covered, well ... *nothing*.

Adam and Eve didn't seem to mind. I imagine them happily skipping through a garden of overgrown tulips on a random Tuesday as they chased a stray zebra. Their privates were swinging and swaying until their nude bodies collapsed on a lush bed of green meadow, and their heart rates returned to normal.

Apparently, they didn't need Benadryl, Claritin, or underpants. Eden was perfect—just as God intended—until that fateful day when sin's shadow arrived on the scene, and Adam and Eve's world changed forever.

Think about it: Adam held no secrets from Eve. Eve hid no Spanx from Adam—no coverings at all. The Bible says they were naked and *unashamed*.

I can imagine their nakedness made their sexual encounters easy and efficient. However, because hiding anything from each other was unnecessary, I suspect their nakedness also made them emotionally available to one another. This is the essence of intimacy. As I travel the country speaking, teaching, and coaching on relationships, I usually define *intimacy* as the state of being naked and *unashamed*.

Contrary to popular belief, intimacy and sex are not the same. Intimacy goes beyond sex. It is much more comprehensive. It involves *all* aspects of you, not just the *physical*. You may have heard intimacy described as *into-me-see*. It's a declaration that nothing is hidden or held back. What you see is what you get, quite literally.

PLOT TWIST

If you're familiar with the story of Adam and Eve, then you know their naked nirvana didn't last long. One day, deception knocked on their picturesque door and let itself in. They, and we, were never the same.

Did God really say?

Whenever that question rings in your thoughts, be careful. It's usually a set up. The deceiver is near.

The Bible teaches in Genesis chapter three that the serpent, shrewd and cunning, approached Eve and asked for a rundown of the commands God had given her and Adam. Without missing a beat, she innocently recounted God's words—even adding in a stray command for kicks.

"Did God really say ...?" the serpent asked (Genesis 3:1).

Pause.

Did God really say? Whenever that question comes to mind, be careful. It's usually a setup. The deceiver is near.

23

But Eve didn't know this, so she continued her conversation with the serpent. Before she knew it, fruit juice was dripping from her lips and onto her bare breasts. She savored that fruit so much that she shared it with Adam, and he ate it too (Genesis 3:6).

Suddenly, "At that moment, their eyes were opened, and they suddenly felt shame at their nakedness. So, they sewed fig leaves together to cover themselves" (Genesis 3:7).

Most preachers who teach this story focus on how Adam and Eve hid from God once they sinned. That's true. But before they hid from God, they hid from *one another*. Eve's bare breasts were no longer beautiful; they were now brazen and needed to be covered immediately. It was no longer appropriate for Adam's manhood to dangle fancy-free. Bring on the fig leaves.

What was once innocent and sacred was now indecent and scandalous. The purity of their nakedness was now tarnished. So, they hid from each other, and *then* they hid from God, covering themselves in thick leaves, possibly from the tree that bore the fruit they'd just consumed. However, it wasn't only their nakedness that prompted them to hide. It was also their sin.

SHAME ENTERS THE SCENE

Before long, God arrived in the garden for the trio's daily walk and talk. But Adam and Eve were nowhere to be found.

"Then the LORD God called to the man, 'Where are you?'" (Genesis 3:9).

Can we pause right here, long enough for me to repeat God's question to you? Where are *you*?

Are you, like Adam and Eve, in a state of hiding? Do past mistakes, fears, unforgiveness, or trauma stand between you and your desire to know your spouse truly? Do you mask your true feelings, sugarcoat your words, or pretend with a forced smile that everything's okay while your heart is breaking into pieces?

Where are you?

Adam's next confession is telling.

"He replied, 'I heard you walking in the garden, so I hid. I was afraid because I was naked'" (Genesis 3:10).

Notice Adam didn't hide from God until he sensed God's *nearness*.

I was coaching a couple last year—we'll call them James and Leslie—who had this very problem. Leslie was a natural empath, wired to feel deeply and connect intimately. She longed, sometimes desperately, to reach James's heart. But his emotional walls were like Fort Knox. No matter what gentle questions she asked or how generously she poured on affirmation, James would not let down his walls and let her in. He wasn't harsh or even rude. He was just … closed.

James, for his part, didn't see a problem. Working double shifts left him drained, and by the time he got home, he felt like he had nothing left to offer. He insisted he just didn't have much to say. Besides, he believed he and Leslie were doing just fine—better than most couples he knew. To him, the reasons he gave weren't excuses. They were just the facts, and they explained the space between them well enough.

Interestingly, when Leslie pursued James, he pulled further away. He wouldn't return her text messages, and on the weekends, he'd zone out watching hours of TV or spend sunny afternoons piddling around doing yardwork. Leslie felt unseen and unimportant. She couldn't understand why James kept pushing her away.

"I think he's having an affair," she blurted out in our one-on-one conversation. "Why else would he be so distant?"

Through the camera lens on my computer, I could see the tears pooling in Leslie's eyes, and before long, her heaviness of heart barreling down her cheeks like a liquid load.

As a marriage coach, my job isn't to make assumptions or give my opinion. But if I'm honest, the type of distance James and Leslie were experiencing *was* often a bright red flag of infidelity. But before we raced down that road, I wanted to first talk to James and see if he'd open up to me.

As James and I talked privately, he admitted he felt completely inadequate—like no matter how hard he tried, he couldn't give Leslie the love and attention she wanted. He promised me there was no affair; he was simply drowning in the weight of his own disappointment. Losing his job after months of double shifts had gutted his confidence. James worried that if he let Leslie in, she'd see the same failure he saw in himself. Vulnerability felt too risky.

But vulnerability is required for intimacy.

Vulnerability is not weakness. It's not curling up on the couch with your spouse and crying together over sad movies. Brené Brown defines vulnerability as uncertainty, risk, and emotional exposure.[i]

It takes courage to reveal who you truly are to others.

Many people feel as James did toward their spouse and toward God. Total failures. They know God sees and knows everything, yet they still hide.

WHO'S IN YOUR EAR?

God follows up Adam's admission with another question: "Who told you that you were naked?" (Genesis 3:11).

The obvious answer is *no one*. There was no one in the garden other than Eve to tell Adam he was naked. It wasn't a *person* who told Adam he was naked. It was a *thing*—sin. Once Adam and Eve sinned by disobeying God, they realized their actual state, and for the first time, they felt shame.

Who or what is causing you shame?

What stories do you believe about yourself?

Who is in your ear?

Who or what is causing you to hide?

Only when we're ready to be honest about the answers to those questions and pursue the freedom God secured for us will we be released from shame. Then, and only then, will we enjoy the true intimacy God desires for us to have with Him and with one another.

IT'S NOT MY FAULT

Adam didn't follow this advice, though. He was caught, but he wasn't going down without a fight. Instead of repenting of his sin, he blamed.

"The man replied, 'It was the woman *you* gave me who gave me the fruit, and I ate it'" (Genesis 3:12, emphasis mine).

Oh no, he didn't.

My man just blamed God.

Oh, he blamed Eve too, but first he blamed God. Essentially, he said, "God, I was doing just fine down here, but *you* decided I needed a wife. So, it's not *my* fault. She gave me the fruit, and like a good husband, I ate it." **

Listen. There aren't many times I want to shrink back from a Bible verse, but if you grew up in the era before *gentle parenting*—as I did—you're thinking God is about to backhand Adam right here in Genesis 3.

God doesn't slap him, but He pronounces the consequences of their sin. The rest of the story explains how God forever banished Adam and Eve from the garden, the place of their innocence. Also, Eve earned the disdain of every woman who has ever endured the pain of childbirth, and the lying serpent lost his legs.

THE ANTIDOTE

Sin has consequences. When we try to shortcut the process of restoration and pursue a faux freedom apart from God, we stay in our shameful state.

Do you know the antidote to shame?

Repentance.

When we acknowledge we've done wrong and repent—go in a different direction—shame loses its power.

Maybe shame has a grip on you, yet you're thinking, *But I didn't do anything wrong.* Perhaps you were the victim of someone else's wrongdoing. Do you know the antidote for that kind of shame?

Forgiveness.

This is how we recover what was lost in the garden. If we've done wrong, we repent. If we've been wronged, we forgive. Then watch shame lose its power.

God wants you to be naked and unashamed—uninhibited—in your marriage. It was His design from the beginning. What's stopping you from renouncing shame and reclaiming your freedom?

APPLICATION

You can choose a shallow marriage or a sincere one, but you can't have both. Deeply connected marriages don't happen by accident. So, instead of small talk, ask your spouse one question that invites a deeper response (see Conversation Starters below). Share one thing about yourself that your spouse may not know. Come out of hiding. Though the shallow waters may feel safer, the deeper waters are more fun and lead to greater intimacy, trust, and a lasting connection.

CONVERSATION STARTERS

1. Where has shame held you back?
2. On a scale of one to five, where one means *not at all*, and five means *completely*, how vulnerable are you?
3. What's one way I can help you move closer toward a five?
4. What is your greatest fear or your greatest hope for our marriage?
5. What do you think is the purpose of your life?

REFLECTION

When Adam and Eve hid in shame, God came looking for them, and He covered them. What does this reveal about His heart toward you when you fail? How might this change the way you respond to God in your own moments of guilt, regret, or shame?

PRAYER REQUESTS

_____

_____

_____

_____

_____

_____

PRAYER

Father God, we come to you not knowing exactly what to do. We want to recover the innocence of our marriage and live intimately, as you designed us to. Where there have been past hurts, give us the grace to repent and forgive. Help us see each other rightly. Give us the courage to open our hearts to one another and the compassion to accept what we see without judgment or rejection. Walk with us like you did with Adam and Eve. Show us the way. In Jesus's name, Amen.

2

Abraham and Sarah:
Faith not Sight

Trusting God's Timing When the Promise Feels Impossible

Then the LORD said to him, "… for you will have
a son of your own who will be your heir." Then
the LORD took Abram outside and said to him,
"Look up into the sky and count the stars if you
can. That's how many descendants you will
have!" And Abram believed the LORD, and the
LORD counted him as righteous because of his
faith.

Genesis 15:4–6

Oh, Abraham.

He started so well.

The first time God tested Abraham's faith, he passed
with flying colors. Earlier in Genesis, we read, "The LORD
had said to Abram, 'Leave your native country, your

relatives, and your father's family, and go to the land that I will show you'" (Genesis 12:1).

Try that on for size.

Would you leave your family, home, job, 401(k), air fryer, and furry friends to go to a land God would *show you*? Mind you, Abraham had no GPS or Siri to guide him, not even a nosy Alexa to take his mind off his troubles. But off he went. And as the story goes, God richly blessed his obedience, giving him much more than he'd ever enjoyed or imagined in his father's house.

Now, a second test: God made another promise. Although the Lord had provided him with great riches, esteem, and other blessings, Abraham had no heir. In a culture where having a son meant legacy and honor, he longed for one with all his heart.

But everything changed when Abraham heard God's voice again. God had been faithful to lead him to the land of Canaan; surely, He would prove faithful and fulfill this new promise of a son to him now.

What you may or may not know is that Abraham (then called Abram) was seventy-five years old when God first promised him a son. His wife, Sarah (then called Sarai), was sixty-five. Now, other than Janet Jackson, who had a baby at fifty, most women I know are not thrilled with the prospect of carrying a child after midlife. Not only is nature in opposition to this, but by that time in life, we're just plain tired! I cannot imagine chasing a tyrannical toddler who stole my dentures from my nightstand. Can you? Even in biblical times, having a child at this age and stage of life was improbable and literally inconceivable.

But Abraham believed God.

I imagine the promise of a son was thrilling until Abraham and Sarah remembered their huge limitations: they were too old to have children naturally. Well, technically, *Sarah* was too old. Men can father children until their dying day. Women, on the other hand, have a ticking time clock until nature takes its course and their eggs fall into the abyss, never to be seen or heard from again.

As Abraham revealed God's promise to Sarah, her multitasking brain went to work. She knew just what to do. God needed some help, and she was the woman for the job. She wouldn't be pushy; just a little nudge would do. Sarah rubbed her hands together as her plan began to take shape. Abraham could sleep with her servant, Hagar, and *that* child would be the promised heir.

Now Sarai, Abram's wife, had not been able to bear children for him. But she had an Egyptian servant Hagar. So Sarai said to Abram, "The LORD has prevented me from having children. Go and sleep with my servant. Perhaps I can have children through her." And Abram agreed with Sarai's proposal. So Sarai, Abram's wife, took Hagar the Egyptian servant and gave her to Abram as a wife … So Abram had sexual relations with Hagar, and she became pregnant.

Genesis 16:1–4

GET OUT OF THE WAY

Have you ever tried to help God out? How did that work out for you?

If you're anything like me, it doesn't go so well when I get in God's way. We, humans, have the best intentions. We really do, but we need to sit down somewhere and let the Lord do what He does best: work. Or, shall I say, be still and know that He is God (Psalm 46:10).

We won't focus in this chapter on the monstrous mess that Sarah and Abraham's *jump-start plan* created (its effects are still felt in the Middle East, between the warring nations descended from Isaac and Ishmael). However, it's essential to emphasize that *faith does not require your strategies.*

I want to give this elderly couple some credit here. Abraham and Sarah could have chosen *not* to believe God. They could have laughed (Sarah certainly did later). They could have scoffed, rolled their eyes, and ignored God's promise. But for twenty-five years, they waited.

And waited.

And waited.

For twenty-five long years.

That should encourage you today. I'll bet that most people have not been waiting on God to come through for twenty-five years! And if you have been, your faith is pure gold.

So, what do you do when you have a promise but zero evidence?

You see through faith what your natural eyes cannot see.

And then you choose to trust God.

Shaun and I have a wooden wall hanging in our bedroom with the words of 2 Corinthians 5:7 (ESV): *For we walk by faith, not by sight.*

I often stare at that wall hanging to remind myself every time my faith gets shaky, and I'm begging God for *a sign* to feed my hope in His promises.

THIRTEEN YEARS OF WAITING AND WARRING

I may not know what it's like to wait on God for twenty-five years, but I have felt the ache of waiting a long time. I felt like I was in a constant war zone with my husband. Our marriage was in shambles. For thirteen years, I prayed for restoration before God finally healed it.

For thirteen long years, I didn't see a thing. Well, maybe a *little* thing here or there. But I certainly did not see any *real* change.

You know how it is—two steps forward and ten steps back. It seemed the more I prayed for my marriage, the worse things got. Our union had been wrecked by infidelity. From the day we said, "I do," neither Shaun nor I practiced boundaries or wisdom, and in time, both of us committed adultery (see chapter nine). Mine was a one-time thing (no excuses; it was still wrong). But Shaun couldn't seem to curtail his cycle of cheating.

I'd find out about another affair.

He'd promise it was nothing.

I'd forgive him.

He'd be good for a few months.

I'd find out about another affair.

He'd admit he'd messed up.

I'd forgive him, then threaten divorce.

He'd be good for a few months.

I'd find out about another affair ...

Are you dizzy yet? Lord knows, I sure was.

I knew my way of handling things wasn't working. But something kept me hanging on. If I'm honest, it wasn't 100 percent faith. My resolve was tangled with fear, stubbornness, and a need for control.

But God doesn't need you to have perfect faith for Him to perform a miracle.

THE FAITH THAT IS REQUIRED

There's a story in the Gospel of Matthew where Jesus's disciples tried—and failed—to exorcise a demon from a boy. I imagine them flinging holy water at the spirit, flipping through the Torah for the secret code, and shouting prayers to anyone who might be listening.

What they couldn't do, Jesus did.

"Why couldn't we cast out that demon?" they asked in dismay (Matthew 17:19).

Jesus replied, "Because of your lack of faith. I tell all of you with certainty, if you have faith like a grain of mustard seed, you can say to this mountain, 'Move from here to there,' and it will move, and nothing will be impossible for you" (Matthew 17:20, ISV).

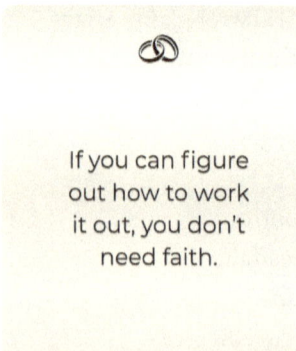

If you can figure out how to work it out, you don't need faith.

Apparently, the disciples had a little Sarah in them. (Don't we all?) They tried to accomplish what could only be achieved by faith with their own strategies.

If you can figure out how to work it out, you don't need faith.

If you need $5,000 to pay a medical bill and you have $5,015 in your bank account, you don't need faith. You simply go to the bank and withdraw the money. But if you need $5,000 and your account shows a –$115 balance, you're going to need some faith. Your bank card will not work.

Faith is the currency in the kingdom of God.

"And it is impossible to please God without faith" (Hebrews 11:6).

When you know the nature and character of God, you trust Him.

For years, my best friend and I have regularly shared stories of God's faithfulness.

We have a saying we tell each other: "We've got history with God." It's true. I could write an entire book on the many ways God has fulfilled His promises to me (and maybe I will!). He has proven Himself trustworthy time after time.

What about you?

Do you and God have history?

Can you look back and remember times when you had nothing but mustard-seed faith, and He came through for you anyway? When your back was against the wall, and He made a way out of *no way!*? When you were at your wits' end, and God was only beginning?

God is faithful! He keeps His promises. Every. Single. Time.

Whatever you're facing individually or as a couple, take a lesson from Abraham and Sarah. It may take twenty-five years, but if God said it, that settles it.

I love how the Contemporary English Version translates this verse: "At the time I have decided, my words will come true. You can trust what I say about the future. It may take a long time, but keep on waiting—it will happen!" (Habakkuk 2:3 CEV).

I don't like to wait, and I'm guessing you don't either. But what happens when we wait on God? Our faith is strengthened, and in time, we see seedlings of patient endurance growing in our lives. The apostle James puts it this way: "For you know that when your faith is tested, your endurance has a chance to grow. So let it grow, for when your endurance is fully developed, you will be perfect and complete, needing nothing" (James 1:3–4).

Twenty-five years after the promise, Sarah finally became pregnant—no surrogate needed—and gave birth to a son, whom she and Abraham named Isaac.

The name Isaac means *he will laugh* or *laughter*.

Listen to how the prophet Jeremiah describes the overwhelming feeling of a promise fulfilled: "I will turn their mourning into joy. I will comfort them and exchange their sorrow for rejoicing" (Jeremiah 31:13).

Though Jeremiah's words had yet to be written in Sarah's day, after more than two decades of waiting, she held a squiggly little baby in her arms—the promise fulfilled. She named him after her response to God's promise—*laughter*.

Imagine the joy that awaits you, too, when God fulfills His promise to you. Can you feel it? Sense it? Touch it, even now by faith? Close your eyes. Your natural sight won't do. See by faith what only God can do.

And when doubt and dismay come knocking, let that hope be the one who answers.

APPLICATION

Believing God when you don't see a thing is an opportunity to choose faith over feelings and promises over proof. As a couple, you can practice this by finding pertinent promises in the Bible and saying them aloud together, even if your circumstances don't agree. Write them on your bathroom mirror—text reminders to each other.

Instead of focusing on what's going wrong, thank God in advance for how He's making it right. Believe He's already working behind the scenes. When doubts creep in, remind each other of past prayers He's answered and victories He's already brought you through. Make it a habit to pray together, declaring, "Lord, even when we can't see you working, we believe you're working."

CONVERSATION STARTERS

1. What is one area in our lives right now where we need to trust God more?
2. Can you share a time when you saw God come through for us in the past, even when it seemed impossible at first?
3. What's a promise from Scripture that feels hard to believe right now?
4. How can we remind each other to choose faith over fear when our circumstances feel discouraging?

5. What would it look like for us to praise God in advance before we see the answer?

REFLECTION

What does God's faithfulness to give Abraham and Sarah a son—despite doubt and delay—teach us about His timing and His nature when our prayers feel unanswered?

PRAYER REQUESTS

_____

_____

_____

_____

_____

_____

PRAYER

Lord, we admit that our faith is weak at times. We want to trust you, but we don't always. Right now, we need help believing you for _____. We won't depend on a sign, but please strengthen our faith. Help us to remember the many times you've come through for us in the past. Help us encourage one another when our faith is weak. We believe your promises are true and your Word does not fail. So, Lord, like the father of the demon-possessed son in Mark chapter nine, we declare, "We believe, help us overcome our unbelief." In Jesus's name we pray, Amen.

3

Isaac and Rebekah: Parenting Fails

Loving Your Children Without Losing Your Unity

And the LORD told her, "The sons in your womb will become two nations. From the very beginning, the two nations will be rivals. One nation will be stronger than the other; and your older son will serve your younger son." And when the time came to give birth, Rebekah discovered that she did indeed have twins! The first one was very red at birth and covered with thick hair like a fur coat. So they named him Esau. Then the other twin was born with his hand grasping Esau's heel. So they named him Jacob. Isaac was sixty years old when the twins were born. As the boys grew up, Esau became a skillful hunter. He was an outdoorsman, but Jacob had a quiet temperament, preferring to stay at home. *Isaac loved Esau* because he enjoyed eating the wild

41

> game Esau brought home, *but Rebekah loved Jacob.*
>
> Genesis 25:23–28 (emphasis mine)

"Mommy, do you have a favorite?" Collin, my youngest child, five years old at the time, was dribbling his basketball on my newly mopped floor when he stopped mid-dribble to ask me this question.

I wondered how long the question had been on his mind. The way his eyes stayed fixed on me, as if waiting for the right opening, told me this wasn't a spur-of-the-moment thought.

I had just pulled our lasagna from the oven and was reaching for dinner plates in a kitchen cabinet. I put my hands on my hips and turned again to face him, a slight smile lifting my lips. My sweet baby boy. Everything he did and said was just so darn cute!

"No, Collin, I love all you kids the same." My words were melodic and matter-of-fact.

"Oh." Collin exhaled a groan dripping with disappointment. "Well, if you did, I think it would be me."

Like ghosts, my other three kids, ages seven, twelve, and fifteen, magically appeared in the kitchen, pointing and talking over each other.

"I told you!"

"See, even Collin knows he's the favorite!"

"What now, Mom? Your little pookie wookie bookie told on you!"

Their speculative statements dripped with triumph. They were convinced they had finally caught me like a bird in a trap.

Shaun wasn't much help either. He just laughed, shaking his head as he set the napkins on the table and gave me a knowing look.

I rolled my eyes and shooed the troublemakers away.

It was the unending argument in our house. The three older kids were convinced that Collin had special privileges they didn't. You couldn't tell them he wasn't my favorite. They thought they had receipts, gladly presenting their evidence whenever they didn't get their way—but he did. For example, if Collin didn't get in trouble for talking back, or if I gave in to his whining for another piece of candy.

As parents, we don't mean to show favoritism. But truthfully, it's usually the kid who is most like us—the one we have the most in common with—that we tend to prefer, even if we don't realize it.

Collin and I are both the youngest in our families. We're both homebodies who love to burn the midnight oil and sleep in well past dawn. We both have peaceful demeanors and are generally unbothered by what other people think of us. We laugh at each other's corny jokes and sing opera off-key around the house until the other family members scream at us to stop. Collin just gets me. But he is not my favorite. No matter what my other kids say.

Jacob and Rebekah had a similar problem.

They had fraternal twin boys who were different in nearly every way. Esau was an outdoorsman who loved to hunt and was probably very adventurous. He was the kind of kid who skinned his knees jumping out of trees while hunting deer with his dad. Jacob, on the other hand, was quiet and likely helped his mother garden or made up stories as he lay on the ground staring up at the stars while she crocheted a blanket nearby. He likely had a clean room and offered to help with the dishes once Rebekah finished cooking.

Can you see where this is going?

Throughout their lives, the twins were rivals.

Because they were boys, they likely craved their father, Isaac's, affection and attention.

Perhaps Rebekah sensed that little Jacob felt left out when Isaac and Esau boisterously reminisced about their wild hunting adventures. Maybe she overheard Esau accuse Jacob of acting like a girl because Jacob disliked loud noises and would scream at the sight of a deer hanging upside down just outside their tent. So, Rebekah did what most moms would do. She took her little pookie wookie bookie under her wing and made sure he felt just as loved.

Years passed, and Isaac's eyesight was failing. Believing the end of his life was near, he resolved to bestow the paternal blessing upon Esau. This blessing was what every firstborn son during that era longed to receive—the spoken, covenantal pronouncement of a promised future. Though Esau had already forfeited his birthright (for a bowl of lentil soup — see Genesis 25:29–34), Isaac still intended to bless him. So, Isaac sent Esau into the fields to hunt and prepare his favorite dish. Afterward, he planned to pronounce the blessing over Esau, just as it should be.

But Rebekah overheard what Isaac had said to Esau and devised a plan of her own. Her baby, Jacob, would not be left out. She waited until Esau left to hunt before quickly springing her plan to life. She convinced Jacob to bring her two goats so she could prepare Isaac's favorite meal. Meanwhile, she instructed Jacob to dress in Esau's clothes and put on the goatskins to mimic Esau's hairy arms.

The plan was foolproof. And it worked! Instead of pronouncing the blessing over Esau, Isaac unknowingly bestowed it on Jacob. Just then, Esau came back home from his hunting trip and presented his father with the meal he'd prepared. But Isaac's hunger wasn't the only thing that had vanished; so had the blessing. It was then that Isaac realized he'd been tricked.

Unfortunately, the blessing he gave to Jacob was irrevocable, and the only words Isaac had left for Esau were to declare that Esau would live by his sword and serve his brother (Genesis 27:40).

Can you imagine the rage vibrating through Esau's body in that moment?

Rebekah could.

She knew both her sons, and she knew Esau would plot to kill Jacob, so she ordered Jacob to flee at once to her brother Laban in Paddan-Aram, a faraway town, until Esau cooled off. As the story goes, it would be over twenty years before Jacob returned home, this time with his own family in tow. But sadly, Rebekah had died and never saw her favorite son again.

As parents, we can learn so many lessons from Isaac and Rebekah's *parenting fails.*

As much as we try to remain neutral, we must guard our hearts against favoring one child over another and against allowing our children to disrupt the unity of our marriage.

I recorded an episode for my *Rebuilding Us* podcast some years ago entitled, "How Putting Your Kids First Harms Your Marriage." You can listen to it at danache.com/marriage-podcasts/159.

The comments I received from that episode were telling. Many parents—mostly moms— believe their kids should come before their marriage. This is a grave mistake. Your children will be grown and gone one day, and if you've prioritized them over your spouse, get ready for trouble.

Gray divorces (when a couple divorces around the age of fifty or has been married for twenty-plus years) are on the rise year after year. The main culprit? Couples are now empty nesters who no longer know each other. They've prioritized their kids while neglecting their marriage.

How many of the arguments between you and your spouse are related to your children, including disagreements about how you raise them? How often do you allow your children to interrupt you and your spouse while you're talking? Do you and your spouse spend a lot of time apart tending to your children's overly busy schedules? Do any of your children feel that they are the favorite? Do your children often pit one spouse against the other?

These are all critical questions to consider as you realign your priorities. Next to God, your spouse should be the most

> Next to God, your spouse should be the most important person in your life.

important person in your life. And your spouse should know it. So should your children.

I remember a time when our daughter, Cayla, was around ten years old. She was complaining because Shaun and I were leaving her and her brothers at home while we went out on *yet another date.* (How dare we?!)

"You love Daddy more than me," she protested, arms folded tight in a dramatic pout.

"Of course, I love Daddy more than you," I replied. "I've known him longer."

Though quippy, my response was true. We always taught our kids that they came second to our marriage, not the other way around. You would be wise to do the same. This also applies to adult children. They still need to know their proper position in the family order.

Years later, Cayla, now a young adult, sent Shaun and me a text one night that made both our hearts swell. It read, "Thank you for showing me what a godly and loving example of a marriage is. I know I complained when I was little because you'd go out on your little dates, (She had to throw in that jab.), but I love that ya'll did that."

Turn on the tears!

What will your children say of *your* marriage when they're grown and gone? Live in such a way that they, too, can say, "You showed me what a godly marriage was all about and didn't make me the center of your world."

APPLICATION

As parents, it's easy to favor one child over another, unintentionally. But showing partiality can create division within the family. Instead, practice affirming each child's unique strengths and giving each child equal opportunities for your loving attention (especially the children who are most different from you).

At the same time, remember that one of the greatest gifts you can give your children is a strong marriage. Putting your relationship first doesn't mean neglecting your kids; it means modeling unity, boundaries, and commitment so they feel secure. Make it a priority to check in with each other regularly, pursue unity in your parenting decisions, and carve out consistent kid-free time to nurture your marriage. Remember, a healthy marriage is the foundation of a healthy family.

CONVERSATION STARTERS

1. Do you ever feel like one of our kids gets more of my attention than the others? How can I do better at balancing that?

2. What's one way we can intentionally show each child that they're equally loved and valued?

3. When was the last time we disagreed about parenting, and how did it affect our unity?

4. What do you think each of our children needs most from us right now, individually?

5. What are some small, everyday ways we can remind the kids that our marriage comes first?

REFLECTION

In what ways does God's sovereignty challenge us to trust Him with our children's futures, rather than trying to control outcomes through favoritism, manipulation, or overcompensation?

PRAYER REQUESTS

_____

_____

_____

_____

_____

_____

PRAYER

Father, you are the greatest example of what it means to love your children unconditionally without favoritism (Romans 2:11). We have made many mistakes in our parenting. Teach us how to love our children well while prioritizing our marriage. Forgive us for the times we've gotten the order confused. Help us to be unified in our decisions, even when we disagree. Show us ways to help any of our children who might be struggling, feeling unloved or unimportant, and guide us in building them up so they can accomplish the plans you have for their lives. In Jesus's name, Amen.

PART 2

Purpose and Passion

4

Jacob and Leah:
Unseen and Unloved

Discovering God's Affection in the Face of Human Rejection

Now Laban had two daughters. The older daughter was named Leah, and the younger one was Rachel. There was no sparkle in Leah's eyes, but Rachel had a beautiful figure and a lovely face. Since Jacob was in love with Rachel, he told her father, "I'll work for you for seven years if you'll give me Rachel, your younger daughter, as my wife." "Agreed!" Laban replied. "I'd rather give her to you than to anyone else. Stay and work with me." So Jacob worked seven years to pay for Rachel. But his love for her was so strong that it seemed to him but a few days.

So Laban invited everyone in the neighborhood and prepared a wedding feast. But that night,

> when it was dark, Laban took Leah to Jacob, and he slept with her.
>
> But when Jacob woke up in the morning—it was Leah! "What have you done to me?" Jacob raged at Laban. "I worked seven years for Rachel! Why have you tricked me?"

Genesis 29:16–20, 22–23, 25

In the last chapter, we discussed the sibling rivalry between Esau and Jacob. Now, we're introduced to two sisters who'd be married to Jacob. He seems to be at the scene of many rivalries (He, too, would later have a favorite son).

After fleeing his brother's wrath, Jacob ended up at his Uncle Laban's (Rebekah's brother) house. Laban agreed to let him live there if he tended the sheep. One day, Laban's younger daughter Rachel caught Jacob's eye, and it was love at first sight. Jacob had to have her. He asked for permission to marry her, and Laban agreed ... if Jacob would work for him for seven years. Easy breezy lemon squeezy. Jacob said yes before Laban even finished his sentence.

In biblical times, it was customary to marry the older child off before the younger. So, at the wedding, since Leah was older than Rachel, Laban gave Leah to Jacob instead. The problem was that Laban conveniently omitted this small detail in his conversation with Jacob.

Imagine with me what the morning after must have felt like for Leah. She had been given in marriage to a man she did not really know. One who did not choose her nor love her. Sure, she'd seen Jacob hard at work on her father's farm, but he always seemed to have eyes for her younger sister, Rachel, not her. Her female cousins and servants even made up silly songs about how Jacob would light up at the sight of Rachel. Nonetheless, one night, her father told Leah to bathe, put on some perfume, and wear her best dress, for she was to be Jacob's bride.

Leah's heart skipped a few beats. She'd dreamed of her wedding day since she was a young girl, but no man had ever pursued her. Could it be her lazy eye that kept suitors at bay? Or maybe it was that she lacked Rachel's curvaceous figure that had every man in Paddan-Aram drooling with desire whenever Rachel walked by.

As the wedding procession music played, Leah's heart danced with delight. It was finally happening for her. She gazed at her soon-to-be husband beneath the shadow of her darkened veil. She wasn't sure what had changed Jacob's mind, but for tonight, she wouldn't worry about all that.

The night went surprisingly well. Jacob was very tender and passionate toward Leah, and she felt new, powerful sensations rushing through every inch of her body as he caressed her longingly. Perhaps he did have eyes for her, too, even if he never showed it. She'd once confided to Rachel that she thought Jacob was the most handsome man she'd ever seen. Maybe, just maybe, he could love her, too, and look at her the way he looked at Rachel.

As the sunlight peered through the open slit in their tent the next morning, Leah propped up on one elbow to gaze at her new husband. She ran her finger down the bridge of his nose. His skin was smooth beneath her fingertips. He lacked the hardened edges she expected, and a smile curved her lips as vibrant memories of last night's passion session flooded her mind. She scooted closer to her man and kissed his lips. He stirred about before opening his eyes to meet her gaze.

Just then, Jacob jolted up from their plush pallet on the floor and screamed. On instinct, Leah yanked the covers around her body and frantically searched for the rodent or large spider that must've horrified her new husband.

"You?" Jacob lurched to his feet. "How did *you* get in here?" He grabbed his pants with shaking hands to cover his nakedness.

Leah's eyes widened as she searched his face, desperate for some sign she had misunderstood.

"I—uh, we are married. I—"

"No! *We* aren't married!" Jacob shook a finger at Leah. "You're not Rachel. You're supposed to be Rachel! Where is my wife, *Rachel*?" His voice trembled as he paced back and forth.

Leah clutched the blanket tighter around her chest as realization crashed into her thoughts. He did not choose her. Her father had tricked Jacob—and her! She thought Jacob had willingly agreed to marry her. But this ...

"You need to leave right now," Jacob's words pierced her thoughts. "I don't know what sick trickery your father is up to, but I don't want you," he said matter-of-factly.

Blood rushed to her ears. The room seemed to shrink as she stood frozen, exposed. Hot tears spilled down Leah's cheeks as she groped around the barely lit tent for her bridal veil. She haphazardly placed it on her head, Jacob's mean words playing like a broken record player in her ears. She quickly slipped on her tunic, leaving her wedding gown behind. With clenched fists, she fought off the tears that were falling rapidly down her face. She moved as fast as she could, putting as much distance as possible between her and this mean man who'd just broken her heart as she bounded for the opening of the tent and into the pale morning light, humiliated and horrified.

SECOND FIDDLE

Have you ever experienced a time when you felt like a second fiddle in your marriage? Perhaps you discovered that your spouse wanted to marry someone else, but they *settled* for you. Or maybe your spouse had an affair, and though they promised it was really *nothing*, you now feel like the other woman or the other man.

Leah was not Jacob's first choice, because she was not beautiful. The Bible describes her as having weak eyes. The Greek word for "weak" in this context is *asthenés* (ἀσθενεῖς), meaning feeble, sick, lacking strength, or helpless.[ii] Leah most likely had an eye condition; she may have been cross-eyed, which diminished her beauty. Rachel, on the other hand, had bright, beautiful eyes and a lovely figure. In essence, Rachel had it going on, while Leah would make a great aunt someday.

Laban eventually gave Rachel to Jacob, albeit requiring him to work *another* seven years

God sees you.
He loves you.
And He can make
you fruitful in the
midst of your
struggle.

to acquire her. So now Jacob had two wives: one he loved, the other he loathed. Throughout their marriage, Leah would play second fiddle to Rachel.

Even though Jacob did not love Leah and likely treated her more like a servant than a wife, God loved her. "When the LORD saw that Leah was unloved, he enabled her to have children, but Rachel could not conceive" (Genesis 29:31).

I want to speak directly to those who feel unseen and unloved by their spouse. God sees you. He loves you, and can make you fruitful even in the middle of your struggles.

THE RIGHT PRIORITIES

Read the following scriptures closely:

> So Leah became pregnant and gave birth to a son. She named him Reuben, for she said, "The LORD has noticed my misery, *and now my husband will love me*." She soon became pregnant again and gave birth to another son. She named him Simeon, for she said, "*The LORD heard that I was unloved* and has given me another son." Then she became pregnant a third time and gave birth to another son. He was named Levi, for she said, "*Surely this time my husband will feel affection for me*, since I have given him three sons!" Once again Leah became pregnant and gave birth to another son. She named him Judah, for she said, "*Now I will praise the LORD!*" And then she stopped having children.
>
> Genesis 29:32–35 (emphasis mine)

Notice that every time Leah had a son, she looked to Jacob to love her. After Reuben was born, Jacob still felt no affection for her. So, she tried again. When Simeon was born, she thought God must be avenging her by giving her another son. Now Jacob would finally notice her. When Levi made his appearance in the world, Leah thought, Third time's a charm! Surely after I've given him three sons, Jacob will love me now.

But notice what happened after Judah was born. Leah takes her eyes off her husband and puts them on the Lord. The name Judah is derived from the Hebrew word *Yada* (or Yadah). It means *praise*. It carries the meanings of to know, confession, or thanksgiving.[iii] Leah turned her worry into worship, and it was then that she stopped having children.

Does this mean God punished her? Quite the contrary. I believe that once she refocused her priorities on what truly mattered—worshipping God, regardless of whether she felt loved or important—she stopped seeking validation in what she could *produce*.

Leah may have been second fiddle, but it was through Leah, not Rachel, that the coming Messiah would be born. Let that sink in. People may devalue you, but God has a purpose and plan for your life, far greater than you know.

I wish Leah had remembered this lesson throughout her plight, but if you keep reading Genesis 30, you'll notice she finds herself in yet another rivalry with Rachel. Rachel had been barren all those years, so she decided she'd use her servant girl as a surrogate to produce children with Jacob. Sound familiar?

Leah, who had stopped conceiving, must have thought, *Two can play that game!* So, each gave their servants to Jacob to sleep with (emulating their husband's grandmother, Sarah) to bear even more children. Somewhere along the way, Leah put her eyes back on Jacob, stooping so low as to pay Rachel, in mandrakes, for an opportunity to sleep with Jacob (see Genesis 30:14–16).

If we don't keep our eyes focused on who we are in Christ, we will inevitably focus on who we aren't to others.

Have you ever experienced deliverance from insecurity only to find yourself competing or comparing yourself to others again? I have. And like a drug, it sucks you back in. If we don't keep our eyes focused on who we are in Christ, we will inevitably focus on who we aren't to others.

COVENANT OVER CHEMISTRY

Interesting fact: Rachel later died from complications during the birth of her son Benjamin and was buried on the side of the road as Jacob and his large family traveled from Bethel to Ephrath, now known as Bethlehem (see Genesis 35:16-19).

Bethel means *house of God*. It was where Jacob encountered God in a way that permanently marked him. Ephrath, as it was called then, means *fruitfulness*. Throughout her life, Rachel longed to be fruitful (see Genesis 30:1). Tragically, she would perish before ever reaching the land that bore that name.

Leah, on the other hand, lived many years after Rachel's death and was buried in the family cave, alongside Abraham, Sarah, and the other patriarchs and matriarchs. Before Jacob died, he chose to be buried next to *Leah* (see Genesis 49:29-32).

Rachel had Jacob's heart, but Leah became his home. Once again, it was through Leah's son, Judah, that the promised Messiah—Jesus—would come. God lifted Leah from obscurity and rejection to a place of honor and legacy.

This is not to say that an unloved spouse should settle for whatever they can get. Remember, biblical times were different, and Jacob's marital situation should be looked at as *descriptive, not prescriptive*.

Covenant will outlive chemistry any day. Instead of focusing on how compatible you and your spouse are or aren't, honor your covenant. It will outlive you.

As a couple, you have the chance to build each other up and avoid comparing your spouse to anyone else. This is the person *you* chose, for better or for worse. May your spouse always feel safe and wanted under your loving gaze.

APPLICATION

If you are feeling unloved by your spouse, take heart. God loves you, sees you, and cares about what you're going through. You can trust your feelings to Him. Take encouragement from I Peter 5:7, "Give all your worries and cares to God, for he cares about you." Unlike people, God loves you unconditionally. Instead of withdrawing from your spouse or letting resentment build, express your feelings honestly. Tell your spouse what you need, focusing on "I" statements rather than accusations. For example, "I feel unseen when you ignore my needs. I need to know that I'm important to you." Pray for God to soften your spouse's heart and to protect yours. Remember that your ultimate worth doesn't come from your spouse's attention but from God's unfailing love.

As a couple, you can work on rebuilding closeness by intentionally setting aside time for connection, speaking words of affirmation to each other, and praying together for God to heal the areas where love feels absent. Be careful never to compare your spouse to someone else. A marriage rooted in God's love can grow even during seasons when one or both of you feel unappreciated, unimportant, or unseen.

CONVERSATION STARTERS

1. When do you feel most loved by me, and when do you feel least loved?

2. What's one small thing I could do this week to help you feel more seen and appreciated?

3. Are there areas where you feel I compare you— perhaps to others or even to an ideal?

4. What do you need from me right now to feel more secure in our marriage?

5. How can we both shift our focus from what's missing to the ways God is already working in our relationship?

REFLECTION

What does Leah's story teach us about God's heart for those unseen or unloved?

PRAYER REQUESTS

_____

_____

_____

_____

_____

_____

PRAYER

Lord, we acknowledge that we did not choose you, but you chose us that we might be fruitful (John 15:16). We confess that there have been times when we have not always prioritized each other. There are times when we have compared our spouse to others, even an ideal version of who they should be. Forgive us for not seeing each other the way you see us. Help us, Lord, to be wise with our affection and attention. Protect our marriage from othering. Thank you for bringing us together, and by your grace, keep us together. In Jesus's name we pray, Amen.

5

Deborah and Lappidoth: Gender Roles That Don't Fit the Mold

Leading with Strength and Confidence in Uncommon Circumstances

Then the people of Israel cried out to the LORD for help, for he (Sisera) had 900 chariots of iron and he oppressed the people of Israel cruelly for twenty years.

Now Deborah, a prophetess, the wife of Lappidoth, was judging Israel at that time. She used to sit under the palm of Deborah between Ramah and Bethel in the hill country of Ephraim, and the people of Israel came up to her for judgment.

Judges 4:3–5 ESV

For many Christians, the question of women in ministry still crackles like a live wire—sparking debate, dividing pews, and stirring hearts that beat for the same God.

I was raised in a denomination that gripped the glass ceiling over women's heads like a steering wheel in a sports car. As a very young child, I felt an unfamiliar queasiness in the pit of my stomach every time any woman who spoke in our church was relegated to the side podium on the floor like a five-year-old in a buffet line. Now, as an ordained pastor, my views are obvious. But let's see what God says, shall we?

Deborah was a leader's leader. Her authority came at a critical time in Israelite history. Due to their fickle faithfulness to God's commands, the Israelites often found themselves subjected to foreign oppression. This time, in His great mercy, God heard their cries for help and sent a solution; someone who would not only judge domestic matters but also courageously battle international disputes on their behalf.

- A woman
- A warrior
- A weapon in the hand of the Lord

It's essential to note that the judges typically served in multiple roles. Most biblical translations *first* describe Deborah as a prophet. Only the New Living Translation and a few others describe her first as the wife of Lappidoth. To me, this shows that Deborah had a relationship with God before she had a relationship with her husband. God called her before she was called Mrs. Lappidoth. Her identity was secure in who created her, not in who caressed her.

Some Christian traditions only recognize a woman's role in ministry as a homemaker. You've likely heard that a woman's first ministry is to her husband and children. However, *everyone* is called to prioritize their relationship with the Lord above their family. For both men and women, the Lord is to be our first ministry. Notice I said the Lord, not church work. It's imperative not to conflate the two. When it comes to a woman's role in ministry, we must understand the difference between Christian tradition and godly truth.

DEBORAH'S FIRST MINISTRY

Deborah played a vital role in Israel's history. Before becoming a judge, she was a prophet—one who hears from God and speaks on God's behalf. What a weighty role! God could have chosen anyone for this assignment, but He chose Deborah. Don't miss the uniqueness of her role. She was the first and only woman in Israel's history to serve as a judge. Could God be speaking to modern Christians from the pages of the Old Testament?

If you do a study on the lives of the other judges, you will learn that most had major character flaws:

- Gideon was bound by a stronghold of fear that constantly corroded his courage (Judges 6:11, 27).

- Jephthah treated God like a foreign deity and made a rash vow that cost him the life of his only daughter (Judges 11:29–40).

- Samson was a notorious womanizer whose arrogance, rebellion, and haughtiness cost him his strength, his vision, and his life (Judges 14:1–2, 18; 16:1, 4–31).

67

- Even the great Samuel could not manage his own household well (1 Timothy 3:4). His sons were rebels who took bribes and perverted justice (1 Samuel 8:3).[iv]

But not Deborah. She wasn't perfect, of course, but the scriptures record no moral failures or character flaws in her life. Still, it wasn't lost on the people that she was *a woman*.

During that time, a man named Sisera was the commander of King Jabin's army in nearby Hazor. He had been terrorizing the people of Israel incessantly. When the Lord told Deborah to commission an Israelite military leader named Barak to overthrow Sisera, Barak agreed—but only if Deborah accompanied him (see Judges 4:6–10). What a warrior woman she must have been!

Let's look closer at Deborah's response. Her words reflect the common attitudes toward women at the time.

And she said, "I will surely go with you. Nevertheless, the road on which you are going will not lead to your glory, for the LORD will sell Sisera into the hand of a woman." Then Deborah arose and went with Barak to Kedesh.

Judges 4:9 ESV

Essentially, Deborah told Barak that the credit he would've received for this victory would go to someone *lesser* than him—a woman. In this case, not Deborah herself, but another woman—a foreign woman at that—a woman named Jael (see Judges 4:17–22).

God uses whoever He wants.

A WORD TO THE WOMEN

If you are a woman reading this, there is much application for you. Men, I'll get to you in a moment.

Women, you need to know you are not second-class citizens in the kingdom of God.

Sure, you might not be able to bench press a 300-pound barbell or eat like a kid on Halloween and still maintain a six-pack. However, there are myriad things you can do (the list is long, and my word count is already protesting) that are unique to you. But this isn't a competition. We were created equal in the sight of God.

The irrevocable call of God applies to women and men alike. Just ask Eve (Genesis 1:27–28), Miriam (Exodus 15:20, Micah 6:4), the daughters of Zelophehad (Numbers 27:1–11), Ruth (Ruth 4:11–12), Huldah (2 Chronicles 34:22),

> The irrevocable call of God applies to both women and men alike.

Esther (Esther 9:29), Mary (Luke 1:45–51), Anna (Luke 2:36–38), Priscilla (Romans 16:3, also see chapter 12), and Lydia (Acts 16:14–15, 40). And that's not even half!

What is the call of God on your life, mighty woman of God? Are you walking in His divine purpose for you, or have you allowed your call to be diminished, devalued, or discarded by cultural or religious norms? But it's not always others who devalue your calling, is it? Sometimes it's the woman in the mirror dimming her light so that it won't shine too brightly.

Jesus affirmed women better than anyone. Just take a stroll through the Gospels to see how He honored, protected, included, restored, and trusted women. He also said, "In the same way, let your light shine before others, that they may see your good deeds and glorify your Father in heaven" (Matthew 5:16 NIV). He's talking to you, sis.

Not every woman is called to church leadership, nor is every man, but all are called to lead in the spheres God entrusts to them. From the Garden of Eden onward, God's design has been clear: men and women leading *together*. If God has not capped your calling, neither should you.

It is my hope and prayer, dear sister, that, like the godly women who came before you, you would rise and take your place in the kingdom of God in all the fullness that He prepared for you.

A WORD TO THE FELLAS

Does your wife have a leadership gift? How are you encouraging that in her? I implore you to take your cues from Lappidoth, even though we know very little about him. His name appears only once in Scripture—Judges 4:4 (ESV): "Now Deborah, a prophetess, the wife of Lappidoth ..." He's an obscure figure with no notable accolades or ambitions. Some might even suggest that he was in Deborah's shadow.

Do you ever feel like you live in the gray edges underneath the shadow of your wife's bright light? Are you tempted to compare your accomplishments to hers? Do people often size you up to your wife, insinuate a deficit in your leadership, or, God forbid, in *you*? Do *righteous* people provoke you to *control your woman* or take the reins in your home?

This is my story—or at least it was. I have a public-facing ministry and business. My photos, videos, and voice are all over the internet. I'm an occasional TV show host. I'm an ordained pastor who serves on my church's preaching team. I'm a public speaker. And I'm a soon-to-be best-selling author (C'mon, speak life with me!).

Shaun is none of those things, and he's as happy as a clam in his role. Shaun is a leader, but not a public-facing one, per se. His role has always been more behind the scenes. That is where he thrives. Fortunately, we belong to a healthy church that doesn't pressure him to pray aloud if he's the only man in the prayer meeting. They don't tell him he needs to learn to preach or join the pastoral team. And the only control they expect is self-control. Shaun has learned to take joy in who God made him to be and in who God created me to be.

There is no striving in our marriage because we refuse to engage in it. I'm sure people have their opinions about us—people always have opinions, mind you. But it's God's thoughts that matter, not people's. If you find yourself succumbing to feelings of insecurity because of your wife's role, or worse, if you have tried to stifle or belittle your wife's leadership, it may be time for honest self-examination or to re-evaluate your theological understanding.

Nowhere in Scripture do we see Lappidoth assert himself in the public square because it was "decent and in order."[v] In this case, he would've been *out* of order because that was not the lane God gave him to run in. Lappidoth must have been a secure man, content in serving God in the way best suited for him, while most likely cheering his wife on beside him. I imagine he was a sounding board—a safe place for Deborah to share her burdens and her heart, and I'm sure he covered her in prayer.

A WORD TO THE WISE

Deborah may have been an uncommon leader, but she was anointed and appointed by God. Not only was Deborah a prophet, a wife, and a judge, but she was also a songwriter and poet (see Judges 5). This lady had it going on! She exemplified what is called a multi-passionate woman. Deborah reminds me of the Proverbs 31 woman. Many Christians don't realize that the woman described in this well-known Proverbial chapter is not an archetype to imitate, but an exceptional allegorical description of Lady Wisdom.[vi]

Wisdom creates a peaceful home, not pretentious platitudes. We are called to pursue kingdom culture, not manufactured mantras, denominational decisions, or ostensible obligations. I believe that both Deborah and Lappidoth made peace with their roles inside and outside the home, and this peace spread into a peaceful society. The Bible also states that after God granted the Israelites victory over Sisera, "There was peace in the land for forty years" (Judges 5:31). Through Deborah's wisdom and Lappidoth's example, they led the way.

Let Deborah's story serve as a reminder that true peace begins with understanding and embracing your God-given identity and calling. Approach your path with confidence and courage, and intentionally pursue His plans for your life. Your obedience to your calling will serve as a powerful example to others, inspiring them to lead in their own calling, even when they find themselves leading in uncommon circumstances.

APPLICATION

Deborah's calling and Lappidoth's support helped fulfill God's kingdom purposes. If your spouse is leading publicly, resist the urge to compare or compete and instead celebrate the unique strengths that God has placed in your spouse. Consider naming the expectations you've absorbed about what a husband or wife *should* do and asking whether those expectations come from God's heart or from culture. You can further apply this by choosing to affirm one another's God-given gifts and callings, even when they don't fit traditional or familiar roles.

As you discuss this, ask each other, "How can I support you in what God has called you to do?" Then follow through with tangible actions—whether that's offering encouragement, taking on extra responsibilities, or praying faithfully for your spouse. When you choose to be your spouse's greatest champion, you not only strengthen your bond but also multiply your collective impact for God's kingdom.

CONVERSATION STARTERS

1. In what ways do you feel most supported by me in your calling or daily responsibilities?
2. Is there an area where you would like me to champion you more intentionally or consistently?
3. How can we celebrate each other's strengths without feeling threatened or competitive?
4. What unique gifts do you see in me that I may not fully recognize in myself?
5. How can we make space in our marriage for both of us to pursue what God has called us to do?

REFLECTION

What do you learn about the character of God through Deborah and Lappidoth's story?

PRAYER REQUESTS

_____

_____

_____

_____

_____

_____

PRAYER

Father, thank you for choosing the specific gifts you have given to both my spouse and me. Forgive us for the times we have devalued our gifts, calling, or anointing because of the chatter of others or our own insecurities. Help us, Lord, to be like Deborah and Lappidoth—secure in our story and focused on your glory. Help us model what kingdom marriage looks like. Thank you for my spouse and for your hand in their life. Help me be an asset, not a liability, to what you're doing in and through them. In Jesus's name, Amen.

6

Solomon and the Shulamite Woman: Passionate Sex

Reclaiming Desire as a Divine Expression of Intimacy

You have captured my heart,
my treasure, my bride.
You hold it hostage with one glance
of your eyes,
with a single jewel of your necklace.

Your love delights me,
my treasure, my bride.
Your love is better than wine,
your perfume more fragrant than spices.

Your lips are as sweet as nectar, my bride.
Honey and milk are under your tongue.
Your clothes are scented
like the cedars of Lebanon.

> You are my private garden, my treasure, my
> bride,
> a secluded spring, a hidden fountain.

Song of Songs 4:9–12

There is likely no more misunderstood book of the Bible than the Song of Songs.

From ancient Jewish wisdom to modern Christian teachings, scholars have varying interpretations of this text. Is it a literal love story or an allegorical account of God's love for us? Was the young man described a random shepherd boy drenched in desire or the stately King Solomon himself? Were the lovers married, or were they just hooking up? Was the woman from a city named Shulam, Shunem, or neither? Or was she actually Abishag (King David's virgin concubine)?

The questions concerning the Song of Songs (or Song of Solomon, as some translations refer to it) are endless and almost caused me to skip this book of the Bible entirely in the book you're reading now.

However, even with its metaphorical mysteries, most Christian marriage advice about sex eventually finds its way back to the Song of Songs. So, in keeping with tradition, I am including this chapter and asking for lots of grace for the way I hold many of these interpretations loosely.

One thing I know for sure is that, whether fictional or factual, these lovers were filled with passion. The book opens with the woman as the initiator. And all the fellas said, *Amen*.

> Kiss me and kiss me again, for your love is
> sweeter than wine.
>
> Song of Songs 1:2

Throughout the book, you'll notice that the young woman is not afraid to say what she wants, when she wants it, and how she wants it. She is unashamed of her body and her sexual desires. This couple's lovemaking sessions are so erotic that they'd earn a parental advisory sticker in a heartbeat.

Legend has it that ancient Jewish men were prohibited from reading the Song of Songs until they were married or at least thirty years old. However, there is no consensus on this rule among the different Jewish groups.[vii] In fact, the Song of Songs is recited on various Passover days in Jewish communities. (What?!) Returning to the idea that the Song of Songs is allegorical, devout Jews recite the book as a reminder of God's passionate, covenantal love for his people.[viii]

For the rest of this chapter, I will approach the Song of Songs as a literal example of passionate sex between two married lovers. This is not to say that this is the correct or only interpretation; it is simply the one I am using to make the point I want to make.

THE BEST SEX

You and your spouse should be having passionate sex. I work with many sexually broken and dissatisfied couples and individuals where the sexual integrity of their marriage has been violated by infidelity, insecurity, injury,

The enemy always tries to pervert what God provides.

or indifference. It's apparent to me that the enemy always tries to pervert what God provides.

Sex in marriage is not solely a right; it's a delight.

My heart breaks for the millions of couples who find themselves in sexless marriages, which is defined as having fewer than twelve sexual encounters in a year.[ix] This is not how God intended marriage to be. God created sex to bond the hearts and bodies of covenantal partners for life.

If physical limitations, pain, or impotence prevent you from enjoying this God-given, pleasurable practice, seek help. There is no shame in that. However, beyond cases of physical disabilities, illness, temporary (mutually agreed-upon) fasting, or other rare cases, couples should have thriving sexual encounters together. And Song of Songs paints quite the picture of how to do just that.

I remember the first time I studied the Song of Songs. I was in my early twenties and had been married for less than five years. My eyes were opened to a whole new world! I grew up in purity culture, where we were taught that modest is hottest, missionary style is godliest, and oral sex? *Fuggedaboutit*! Good Christian girls did not do *that*.

We were the same girls who had to wear one-piece bathing suits with shorts and a T-shirt *just in case* a little butt cheek tried to escape and lead the brethren astray.

Because apparently, teenage boys had the self-control of feral raccoons, and my shoulder blade was a spiritual stumbling block waiting to happen.

I always thought the abundance of conversation surrounding what couples do in their bedrooms was excessive and intrusive. But that didn't stop stuffy church folks from talking about it. Speaking of, I have found that when it comes to church conversations about sex, there are two main types: churches that avoid the conversation altogether and churches that seem obsessed with who's sleeping with whom and how. It's rare to hear a sermon that teaches about sex in a normal, open, and healthy way, and sadly, this mishap spills into Christian marriages, too.

As I grew into adulthood, the more I studied, the more I had to unlearn. I realized that the inspired Word of God describes in great detail a heck of a good time with my husband. So, being the good Christian girl that I am, inspired by the Shulamite woman and the God who created her, I made some adjustments, much to Shaun's delight. I wasn't just a hearer of the Word; I became a doer! Bless the Lord.

MEETING YOUR SPOUSE'S SEXUAL NEEDS

I used to say that sex is not a need.

And I was wrong.

Well, kind of.

Though you won't die if you don't have sex, your marriage might.

I remember learning about Maslow's hierarchy of needs in my freshman Psychology 101 class in college. According to renowned psychologist Abraham Maslow, the most basic human needs are physiological (air, water,

79

food, shelter, sleep, clothing, and reproduction).[x] But the higher you climb the hierarchy, the more the needs seem like desires (self-actualization, anyone?).

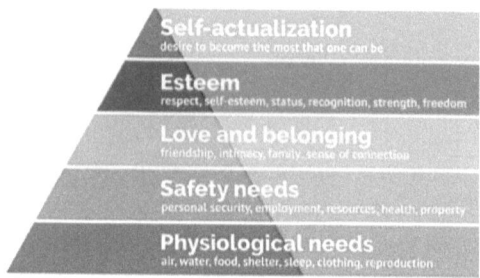

Maslow's hierarchy of needs

©Plateresca / Getty Images

As you can see, sex is not on the list. Some might argue that, although it's not a physiological need, sex can be considered a psychological need. I believe what we're seeking is intimacy. However, sex is *not* intimacy. It's just one of many types of intimacy (e.g., emotional, spiritual, intellectual, and recreational). See my podcast episode "Beyond the Bedroom: 5 Types of Intimacy Every Couple Needs" at danache.com/marriage-podcasts/366 to learn more. Still, sex is the only type of intimacy—the only desire— that *only you* can rightfully meet for your spouse.

Consider this: if your spouse needs emotional support, they can call their best friend for a pick-me-up. Intellectual stimulation? Your spouse can have long talks with their professors or colleagues about facts no one else cares about. Recreational interactions? Any close-knit group of friends will do, and so forth. But who is going to meet your spouse's sexual needs? Tag! You're it. This is why regularly withholding sex from your spouse can harm their emotional health and damage your marriage.

I am convinced that couples who feel sexually inhibited likely have unhealed wounds or unhealthy beliefs. Perhaps your spouse was a victim of childhood molestation and struggles with confidence and shame when it comes to sexual intimacy. Or, as was true for me, religious jargon still echoes in your spouse's mind, even during the act of lovemaking.

What if the wife feels physical pain during sex? Or what if there is so much distance or dysfunction in your marriage that just the thought of making love makes your spouse want to vomit? It's essential to get to the root causes of why sex is lacking. Check to ensure you're not the problem. Be patient with your spouse and offer a compassionate and listening ear. Seek professional help if needed. The reasons for sexual distance in a marriage are many, but the Song of Songs paints a blueprint for how beautiful, adventurous, and pleasurable sex can really be.

MIND, BODY, SOUL

Verse nine of chapter four gives a big clue as to what makes this couple's sex life so intoxicating. It's not just their physical attributes, which they describe in spades, nor is it that they are young, wild, and free. Their *hearts* are

> The best sex is when you know the encounter isn't purely physical, but purposeful; encompassing the mind, body, and soul.

captivated, deeply connected.

The best sex is when you know the encounter isn't purely physical, but purposeful, encompassing the mind, body, and soul.

We live in the age of the hookup—where two strangers can meet, get tingly down there for each other, have sex, and never speak again. The fact that this is seen as normal dating by the younger generation tells us that we've seriously lost our way.

Sex was never meant to be only physical. In Genesis, when God brought Eve to Adam, his first words weren't, "Wow! Look at that rack!" or, "Dang, baby got back!" They were, "At last! This one is bone from my bone, and flesh from my flesh!" (Genesis 2:23).

Adam knew there was something, or someone, missing from his life. Now with Eve on the scene, he felt all the pieces were in place. Eve was God's gift to Adam in every way.

How different would your marriage be if you saw your spouse as God's gift to you? If you approached your marriage bed with more than an orgasm or an obligation on your mind? What if you saw your spouse as an extension of yourself—to have and to hold from this day forward? How might this realization electrify your sex life?

If you wish your spouse were more talkative in the bedroom, try reading the Song of Songs together regularly. Need new physical positions? It's in there, too. Want your wife to initiate sex more often? Remind her of her spiritual Shulamite sister who came before her. In fact, many Christian and Jewish spouses choose to read the Song of Songs together as foreplay. *Ooh la la.*

Let's redeem passionate, purposeful, and phenomenal married sex. Let's reclaim the gift of sex that God designed to bond us to our spouse emotionally and physically. Make your sex life so enjoyable that the next time you're watching a sitcom and the actors joke about their dry, boring sex life, you can look at your spouse and say, "They must be single!"

APPLICATION

Remind yourself that sex is a gift from God to be nurtured, not neglected. This means intentionally expressing your desire through words and actions, staying curious about your spouse, and pursuing each other regardless of how long you've been married. You can do this by setting aside distraction-free time for different types of intimacy, scheduling lovemaking sessions if necessary, writing erotic notes to one another, experimenting together, or simply speaking out loud the qualities you admire in your spouse.

When you choose to delight in one another the way the young man and the Shulammite woman did, you keep the spark of love alive and reflect the physical pleasure God designed for marriage.

CONVERSATION STARTERS

1. How do you feel most pursued by me—through words or actions?
2. What's one new way we could add more romance or playfulness into our relationship?
3. When do you feel most desired by me—what sets the mood for you?
4. What part of my body do you find most attractive, and why?

5. What's one fantasy or intimate experience you'd love for us to try together?

REFLECTION

What truth about God do you learn after reading through the Song of Songs?

PRAYER REQUESTS

_____

_____

_____

_____

_____

_____

PRAYER

Lord, we are so thankful for the gift of sex. We want to see our bodies and each other the way you designed us to see them. Remove the lies, mind blocks, and inhibitions that religion, society, or we have put on ourselves. Bless us with a new sexual freedom toward each other that we have not yet known. Remind us to prioritize this area of our marriage. Protect our marriage from sexual perversion and sexual passivity. Give us eyes only for one another and let us relish in our sexual love. In Jesus's name, Amen.

PART 3

Tension and
Transformation

7

David and Michal:
Love That Grows Cold

Restoring Respect When Resentment Creeps In

In the meantime, Saul's daughter Michal had
fallen in love with David … So Saul gave his
daughter Michal to David to be his wife.

I Samuel 18:20, 27

But as the Ark of the LORD entered the City of
David, Michal, the daughter of Saul, looked
down from her window. When she saw King
David leaping and dancing before the LORD,
she was filled with contempt for him.

When David returned home to bless his own
family, Michal, the daughter of Saul, came out
to meet him. She said in disgust, "How
distinguished the king of Israel looked today,

shamelessly exposing himself to the servant
girls like any vulgar person might do!"

2 Samuel 6:16, 20

I was first introduced to John Gottman's four horsemen of
the apocalypse during a tense marriage counseling
session—my own.

I sat on the sagging blue couch with my arms folded
so tightly around my chest, I must've looked like I was in a
straitjacket. My lips were pursed just as tightly. I shook my
head in disagreement with every word that proceeded out
of Shaun's mouth, though honestly, I wasn't listening to a
word he was saying. All I knew was like Meghan Trainor
sang; his lips were moving, so it must've all been lies, lies,
lies. He had done lord knows what, and I was not having it
this time.

Our therapist looked me over, put his notepad down
on his desk, and leaned in toward me. "Have you heard of
Gottman's four horsemen?" He asked, his tone wavered
between exasperation and compassion.

Maybe I should've been listening to whatever Shaun
was talking about more closely, because clearly the
conversation had ventured off into Never Never Land.

I highly respected John Gottman. His expert
teachings on relationships had carried me through many
seasons of marital upheaval. But the four horsemen? What
the what? What did sci-fi have to do with my lying
husband?

Our therapist took my furrowed brows as
confirmation that I had no idea what he was talking
about, so he went on to explain that four significant
negative communication responses can derail and

eventually destroy a marriage: stonewalling, defensiveness, criticism, and contempt.[xi] He asked if I could identify with any of the four horsemen.

I let his words linger in my mind for a while before blurting out, "I don't have a horseman. I just don't like him!" I threw Shaun a dismissive glance.

My answer cut deep, and I knew it.

Shaun let out a long sigh. We weren't getting anywhere.

Oh well, I had told him I didn't think these counseling sessions were helping anyway. If they asked for my opinion, I was going to give it.

I didn't know it then, but I had a horseman, all right. I was struggling with all four!

Now that I'm a little older and a lot wiser, having taught Gottman's four horsemen to my coaching clients, in my marriage workshops, and on my podcast, I can affirm, Mr. Therapist, that, yes, I did have contempt for my husband. As a matter of fact, my heart was as cold as ice on a wintery hillside, untouched by Shaun's efforts and unbothered by my own missteps.

If you've ever felt disdain toward your spouse because they had the nerve to breathe while you were in the room, you may have a horseman, too. This next biblical couple's story shows how contempt erodes a marriage in full color.

THE WAR OF THE ROYALS

David's life is one of my favorites in all of Scripture. Shortly after he had miraculously killed the giant Goliath, David began his military feats against the Philistines. Just as quickly, he went from being a celebrated commander in

King Saul's army to the object of King Saul's erratic envy. Day and night, King Saul dreamed of David's demise, devising plans to execute his former armor-bearer.

As King Saul grew increasingly obsessed with David, an idea slithered into his mind. He would offer his daughter Michal—who had fallen deeply in love with David—as a "prize" if David killed one hundred Philistines and returned with their bloody foreskins as proof. Yes, your imagination is correct. What a sick challenge. But this giant-slayer was up for the challenge. He saddled his horse and galloped into Philistine territory with Michal on his mind. Whether it was adrenaline or ambition, David went above and beyond and threw *two hundred* Philistine foreskins at the feet of his tyrannical king.

Throughout the rest of King Saul's life, he schemed and strove to have David killed, but David averted every attack. On one such occasion, in the dead of night, King Saul sent a small army to David's home to lie in wait in hopes of ambushing him when he came outside the next morning.

> But Michal, David's wife, warned him, "If you don't escape tonight, you will be dead by morning." So she helped him climb out through a window and he fled and escaped.

1 Samuel 19:11–12

King Saul raged at Michal's audacity to be loyal to her husband. He snatched her from her home and married her off to another man named Palti, discarding the fact that Michal was still a loving and devoted wife to David.

Through no fault of her own, her devious dad dishonored her marriage vows and flippantly gave her away like a trading card to another man. His motive? Spite.

When you look at the meaning of Palti's name, however, a secondary story starts to emerge. Palti means *my deliverance*, *God liberates*, or *escape from the Lord*.[xii] Despite her father bouncing her between men like a human yo-yo, using her as a pawn in his power games, God mercifully delivered Michal.

David was now an outlaw, and Michal would've most likely ended up back in Saul's dysfunctional home. But God used Saul's spite to liberate Michal.

David and Michal would spend approximately ten years apart before being reunited after King Saul's death.[xiii] But it was not a happy reunion. Michal's love for David had grown chilly. Perhaps she had been persuaded by her father's evil lies about David. Or maybe she had settled into her new life with her new man, Palti, before being abruptly removed against her will *again* (2 Samuel 3:14–16) and thrust into the new King David's harem. No longer was she simply David's adoring wife; she was now one of *many* wives.

WHEN CELEBRATION TURNS CAUSTIC

As the new king, David would now secure his throne, rid himself of Saul's family, and fortify his military. But first, he resolved that the Ark of the Covenant—which carried the very presence of God—would be relocated to the new City of David, where it belonged.

After the ark was in its rightful place, King David threw the biggest party the land had ever seen. David was a man after God's heart (1 Samuel 13:14, Acts 13:22), and his priority was to re-establish a place where God's presence and glory would dwell. Now, not only was the kingdom firmly in David's grip, but worship had been restored to the land.

And David danced before the LORD with all his might, wearing a priestly garment.

But as the Ark of the LORD entered the City of David, Michal, the daughter of Saul, *looked down* from her window. When she saw King David leaping and dancing before the LORD, she was filled with contempt for him.

When David returned home to bless his own family, Michal, the daughter of Saul, came out to meet him. *She said in disgust,* "How distinguished the king of Israel looked today, shamelessly exposing himself to the servant girls like any vulgar person might do!"

2 Samuel 6:14, 16, 20 (emphasis mine)

This is what contempt in marriage looks like: looking down on someone in disgust. Gottman further defines contempt as "disrespect, mocking with sarcasm, ridicule, calling someone names, and mimicking or using body language such as eye-rolling or scoffing. The target of contempt is made to feel despised and worthless."[xiv]

Did Michal have the right to be angry? Was she mistreated? Was David's behavior dramatically different from the behavior of his predecessor? I'd say yes to all the above. We can empathize with Michal for how she'd been tossed around like a rag doll. But no matter how we answer these questions, Michal's attitude toward her circumstances was ungodly. Her response to her husband and her king, though understandable, was inappropriate, especially for that time.

"Contempt is the single greatest predictor of divorce and must be avoided at all costs."

John Gottman

How does contempt show up in your marriage? Do you feel justified by your outbursts, cursing, yelling, hurtful sarcasm, or mean words? Have you vilified your spouse at times because of your own pain? Be careful. Gottman warns that "Contempt is the single greatest predictor of divorce and must be avoided at all costs."[xv]

FROM CONTEMPT TO COMPASSION

There will undoubtedly be times in your marriage when you disagree with how your spouse is behaving. A wise spouse will first pray and seek God's timing on addressing the situation, if the Lord has you to address it at all.

My life changed for the better when I realized that God is a much better defender than I am. It's amazing what happens when I choose to tell on Shaun (I mean pray) to God instead of airing all of Shaun's faults to him and anyone else who will listen.

Most often, God softens *my* heart, gives me another perspective, and instead of contempt, compassion fills my heart, dripping meekness instead of meanness on Shaun.

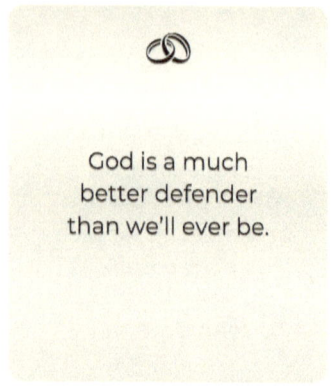

God is a much better defender than we'll ever be.

This happens 79 percent of the time, and the 21 percent where it doesn't is because I'm being stubborn or I've talked to myself about Shaun's mistakes instead of talking to God.

For my own sanity, I created a four-part step-down process from the crazy cycle of contempt. Let me share that with you:

4-PART STEPDOWN PROCESS
away from contempt

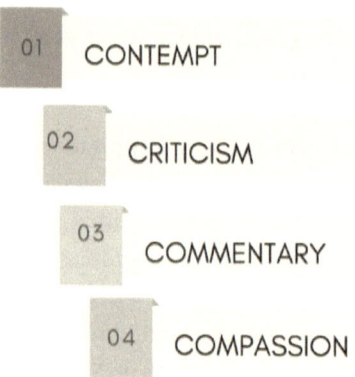

01 CONTEMPT

02 CRITICISM

03 COMMENTARY

04 COMPASSION

There are times when offering a critique or commentary is necessary, and you need to share your perspective on your spouse's behavior. But let it be born from compassion—a sympathetic awareness of another's distress, coupled with a desire to alleviate it—not from contempt. God placed you in your spouse's life for a reason—*to encourage growth.*

> Two people are better off than one, for they can help each other succeed. If one person falls, the other can reach out and help. But someone who falls alone is in real trouble.
>
> Ecclesiastes 4:9–10

What is the motivation behind your critique?

Is it to get your point across? To show your spouse that he is wrong? To win an argument? To make her feel stupid? To help him see the pain he is causing you? To help her grow into the fullness of who God created her to be? To offer another reasonable solution?

I think you know which of these motives Jesus would side with. Shouldn't we follow suit?

Carrying a grudge, which is the *Christianese* way of saying *refusing to forgive*, not only robs you of joy but, like a cancer, it corrupts the good cells of your relationship. Only by allowing the Holy Spirit to help you forgive can you release the toxic trait of contempt in your marriage and position your heart toward compassion.

In the end, Michal's story closes with a somber line: because contempt had taken root in her heart, God closed her womb, and she never bore children (2 Samuel 6:23). It's a tragic reminder that contempt—left unchecked— can choke the very life out of the blessings God longs to give us. Don't let bitterness become the lens through which you see your spouse, yourself, or your God. Guard your heart, keep short accounts, and stay tender before the Lord so that nothing He desires to birth in you is ever hindered by the quiet corrosion of contempt.

APPLICATION

When Michal looked down on David's worship with criticism and scorn, it widened the distance between them that was never healed. When feelings of contempt arise in your marriage, catch them early and replace them with compassion and grace. Instead of criticizing, ask genuine, thoughtful questions. Instead of belittling, look for something to affirm in your spouse. Choose humility over hot takes and ask God for eyes to see your spouse as He does. By practicing honor in both words and attitudes, you can dismantle contempt before it takes root.

CONVERSATION STARTERS

1. Have I ever made you feel dismissed or looked down on? How did it affect you?
2. How can we turn our disagreements into opportunities to understand each other better instead of criticizing?
3. What words or actions from me make you feel most honored in our marriage?
4. Are there any situations where you feel I may still be holding unforgiveness toward you?
5. How can we remind each other that we're on the same team, even when we disagree?

REFLECTION

How do King David and Michal's responses reveal God's concern not only with individual faith, but also with how we treat our spouse when we disagree?

PRAYER REQUESTS

_____

_____

_____

_____

_____

_____

PRAYER

Dear Lord, we admit that we have sometimes held each other in contempt. We choose to forgive past hurts and failures. We choose to release each other from earning our love and respect. Please forgive us for holding bitterness, rage, apathy, a critical heart, or worse, toward one another. Remove our stony hearts and give us tender and responsive hearts (Ezekiel 36:26). Help us see each other through the lens of unconditional love and generous grace. In Jesus's name, Amen.

8

Abigail and Nabal:
When You're Married to a Fool

Maintaining Wisdom and Grace
When Your Spouse Acts in Haste

Then David moved down to the wilderness of
Maon. There was a wealthy man from Maon
who owned property near the town of Carmel.
He had 3,000 sheep and 1,000 goats, and it was
sheep-shearing time. This man's name was
Nabal, and his wife, Abigail, was a sensible and
beautiful woman. But Nabal, a descendant of
Caleb, was crude and mean in all his dealings.

I Samuel 25:1–3

I find it a delightful coincidence that I happen to be
drinking a hot cup of jasmine tea while writing this
chapter, because, honey, I am about to spill all the tea on a
highly unusual and seemingly irreverent story in the Bible.

At the time of I Samuel 25, David was still on the run from King Saul, who had been trying to kill him for nearly fifteen years because envy had taken hold of his heart. In the previous chapter, you read about how low King Saul would go. David was now in yet another hideout and depended on provisions from nearby neighbors who pitied his plight. Though he'd already been anointed king more than a decade prior—that's a story for another day—he had not yet been appointed king of Israel.

David and his men were running low on food and other provisions, and he heard that a wealthy local man named Nabal was simultaneously enjoying an abundance. David remembered a time when he and his men watched over Nabal's shepherds, protecting them from harm, and he figured Nabal would want to return the favor by sharing some of his surplus with David.

But boy, was he wrong.

When David sent ten of his young men to ask for modest provisions to care for all those traveling with him, Nabal scoffed, sneered, and sent them back empty-handed. David was livid. "Get your swords!" He told them (1 Samuel 25:13).

David marched through the wilderness to Nabal's house, no doubt planning his quick and quenchless demise. How dare Nabal return his care for cruelty? He'd see to it that not even one man of his household would be left alive the next morning (1 Samuel 25:22).

IN STEPS WISDOM

Immediately, it seems, one of Nabal's servants went to Abigail to relay the news.

"Abigail wasted no time" (1 Samuel 25:18).

Like a ninja in the night, Abigail sprang into action, quickly assembling the best of her and Nabal's provisions: bread, wine, lamb chops, raisins, fig cakes—you name it.

"But she didn't tell her husband Nabal what she was doing" (1 Samuel 25:19).

I'd love to hear a fundamentalist preacher try to explain that verse. That's right, the Bible says she went behind Nabal's back to protect his back. Abigail was a wise woman. She knew the ramifications of her husband's rash refusal and what it could mean for their entire household, so she did what wisdom does in moments like these. She intervened. Even without her husband's permission.

Abigail moved toward David and his men, unflinching, the weight of her mission steadying her steps. As she approached with her guilt offering in tow, she spoke sensibly and selflessly. She even went as far as to take the blame for Nabal's foolishness upon herself (see 1 Samuel 25:23–31).

Now the tea ... after Abigail presents David with the provisions, listen to how she speaks about her husband:

- "Nabal is a wicked and ill-tempered man."
- "Please don't pay any attention to him."
- "He is a fool, just as his name suggests."
- "Let all your enemies and those who try to harm you be as cursed as Nabal" (1 Samuel 25:25–26).

Dang! I don't think Nabal was Abigail's fave. I also suspect most pastors, Christian marriage coaches, and counselors would not include Abigail's descriptions of Nabal in their advice to wives on how to affirm their husbands. Not exactly how the godly women of old talked about their men, huh? But Abigail was right. Her husband was a fool. In fact, the name Nabal means fool, so apparently, even his parents thought this man was and would always be a fool. How's that for gentle parenting?

But more than her truthful description of her husband, it was Abigail's courage and grace that kept David from unnecessary bloodshed that day. Not only did Abigail assuage David's anger, but she also prophesied his future.

"The LORD will surely reward you with a lasting dynasty, for you are fighting the LORD's battles. And you have not done wrong throughout your entire life" (I Samuel 25:28).

> Even when you are chased by those who seek to kill you, your life is safe in the care of the LORD your God, secure in his treasure pouch! But the lives of your enemies will disappear *like stones shot from a sling!* When the LORD has done all he promised and has made you leader of Israel, don't let this be a blemish on your record. Then your conscience won't have to bear the staggering burden of needless bloodshed and vengeance.
>
> 1 Samuel 25:29–31 (emphasis mine)

This is how you know if you've got a great mate—they not only have grace for your mistakes (see chapter seven), but they also have conviction for your mission. Abigail not only spoke to the David of today, but also to the David of tomorrow. She spoke into David's future, and I believe it was then that David resolved to make this woman his wife one day.

Don't miss the phrase in the scripture *like stones shot from a sling*. Aw, snap! Was Abigail shooting her shot? Recall the story of David and Goliath ... who shot stones from a sling? *David*. It was years prior, though, no doubt the story was still being circulated around town. Maybe Abigail was saying to David, "I know who you are. I've been following your story for a long time." Just sayin'...

Because of Abigail's wisdom, good sense, and excellent persuasive skills, David relented. Lowering his sword, the fury drained from his face. The tension in his shoulders loosened. He signaled his men with a slight nod, and their march halted to a standstill. Instead of payback, he granted peace to Abigail and her fool of a husband.

The story goes on to say that when Abigail returned home, Nabal was holding court in his own dining hall— goblet tipped in his hand, his laughter rattling the rafters. Platters of untouched food surrounded him, and his eyes glazed over as he swayed in his seat—a king in pretense, drunk as a skunk.

Timeout. Ladies, imagine you've just saved your husband's life—rescued him from the consequences of his own foolish choices— only to find him throwing a party for himself, completely oblivious to your sensitivity and sensibility? In modern terms, you saved your husband from becoming a drive-by shooting victim at the hands of a notorious gang, only to watch him race his expensive sports car down the streets of Los Angeles dressed in a red hoodie and bandanna, daring danger to find him again.

We can only imagine how Abigail felt. Nabal's foolish pride had put their entire household in danger, yet here he was celebrating like a king. But because she was wise, Abigail waited to tell Nabal about her and David's exchange until the next day, when he was sober and of sound mind.

The next morning, as Abigail filled Nabal in on the details, the news of what she did so shocked him that he had a sudden stroke, and ten days later, God struck him dead (see 1 Samuel 25:36–38).

Now it's time for David to shoot *his* shot.

When David heard that Nabal was dead, he said, "Praise the LORD, who has avenged the insult I received from Nabal and has kept me from doing it myself. Nabal has received the punishment for his sin." Then David sent messengers to Abigail to ask her to become his wife.

1 Samuel 25:39

And David and Abigail lived happily ever after. Well, not exactly, but justice was served, sure enough.

WHEN YOU'RE MARRIED TO A FOOL

Do not, I repeat, do not look at your spouse, but do you sometimes feel you're married to a fool? Keep your eyes straight ahead, or if you're reading this, keep them glued to the page. Do the decisions your spouse makes cause you to regret the day you said, *I do*? Keep looking straight ahead. Do you ever wonder how the synapses in your spouse's brain sync with conventional common sense?

I can't say whether I feel your pain or not because my husband is also reading this book. I will say, however, that you are not alone.

Many spouses, in an effort to be respectful, find themselves caught between a rock and a hard place when responding to a foolish mate. If you're a woman, it's even harder because of cultural and religious expectations and how biblical submission has been butchered, I mean, taught.

Wisdom is the antidote to foolishness. There's an entire book of the Bible (Proverbs) dedicated to this idea. One such verse is "A worthy wife is a crown for her husband" (Proverbs 12:4). Likewise, a virtuous husband is a gift to his wife. If your spouse struggles with foolish thoughts and decisions, the Lord sees. Remember, God is a much better defender than we'll ever be. He will bring justice to your situation if you trust Him. Pray for wisdom and discernment to know what to do, what to say, and, like Abigail, the proper timing of when and how to take action. And while you're at it, pray that God will help your spouse resist the pride that lurks in the heart and instead walk in humility and make wise decisions.

APPLICATION

This story reminds us that our choices affect not only ourselves but also our spouses and families. In practice, it shows us how to reject pride and stubbornness in conflict and instead follow Abigail's model of wise words and thoughtful action. When tension rises in your marriage, choose to pause, pray, and pursue God's wisdom. Don't just react. Model what it looks like to respond with humility rather than defensiveness and be willing to step in with grace when your spouse is weak. By choosing wisdom over foolishness and humility over pride, you can safeguard your marriage and cultivate a home characterized by peace.

CONVERSATION STARTERS

1. What's one time in our marriage when you think I acted more like Nabal—foolish and stubborn— and how did we work through it?
2. Now, tell me your Nabal moment. Looking back, what's a situation where you realize you weren't thinking or responding wisely?
3. When pride sneaks into our relationship, what's a loving way we can call it out of each other?
4. If we made a foolish spouse survival kit, what would we put in it?
5. How can we protect our marriage and family from the consequences of foolish choices—financially, spiritually, or relationally?

REFLECTION

How does God's intervention in this story remind us that He is able to deal with injustice and protect His people?

PRAYER REQUESTS

_____

_____

_____

_____

_____

_____

PRAYER

Dear Lord, we humbly submit ourselves to you. You are the all-wise God, sovereign and just. We admit our failures and foolishness to you. Many times, we have reacted in fleshly ways instead of responding in faithful ways. Please forgive us. Teach us your character. As you are the Source of all wisdom, lead us by the Holy Spirit into what we need to know and when we need to know it. Please help us to cover each other's weaknesses with your strength. Create in us a clean heart, Oh God, and renew a right spirit within us (Psalm 51:10). In Jesus's name, Amen.

9

Hosea and Gomer: When Your Spouse Is Unfaithful

Choosing Restoration Over Revenge When Betrayed

When the LORD began to speak through Hosea, the LORD said to him, "Go, marry a promiscuous woman and have children with her, for like an adulterous wife this land is guilty of unfaithfulness to the LORD." So he married Gomer daughter of Diblaim, and she conceived and bore him a son.

Hosea 1:2-3 NIV

I remember the day I lost all trust in my husband as if it were yesterday.

I felt a low, hollow feeling in the pit of my stomach as my trembling fingers clicked on an email bearing the name of a woman I'd long been suspicious of.

The room went black as my eyes darted from line to line, taking in the graphic details of what my husband had done when he was out of town that weekend. My eyes grew wider as I read each sordid detail, and the thumping of my heart seemed to vibrate in my ears.

I discovered Shaun's infidelity about a year into our marriage. It had already been a rough season. It seemed we could never find our footing after being repeatedly knocked down by the tsunami-level tidal waves of trials. Not only that, but then add to it the icy looks, cold shoulders, and frigid environment that became all too familiar as we waited each other out after another failed attempt at communication.

I felt the weight of the world grinding into my shoulders like sharp fingernails after I found out. Honestly, I never would have married Shaun if I had known what pain awaited me on the other side of "I do."

To be fair, I wasn't a saint either. I also had an affair around the same time Shaun was canoodling with that woman. Whether my actions were born from retaliation or rebellion, they were still wrong. I was wrecked the morning after. How could I have stooped so low, devaluing myself like an abandoned penny and giving my body to another man? I ended the one-night stand and the one-time friendship the very next day and never looked back. The pleasure was not worth the pain.

Unfortunately, Shaun did not have the same rapid response to his unfaithfulness, and our marriage would stay broken for years due to his cycles of infidelity. It was as if his lustful liberties curled around his ankles like a desperate hand, refusing to let go. He'd repeatedly relapse into adultery after short stints of good behavior. Despite his assurances that boundaries had been restored, small discoveries told a different story. A purchase that raised questions, and the knowledge that the affection I received was being shared. Each discovery reopened wounds I was trying to close.

Another relapse. Another Sunday morning—fresh from church, of all places—I decided I'd had enough.

I rarely curse. But that day I laid into him. I was angrier than I'd ever been. And I didn't hold back. All the years of betrayal and backtracking surged from my broken heart to my throat and poured out of my mouth as every four-letter word I knew flew into the air toward him. The performance left my thoughts scattered, struggling to land anywhere solid.

"I'm sorry," was all Shaun could muster. His voice was barely above a whisper.

When I didn't respond, he turned, head down, and walked out of our bedroom.

I didn't understand why he kept doing this to me ... to us. Everything had been going so well ... or so I thought. My breathing was labored, and my whole body was trembling from the pure rage and sheer exhaustion that had just escaped me.

I wasn't perfect. I had messed up, too. But I stopped. Why couldn't he? Why *wouldn't* he? I felt so stupid for trusting him again. Why did he have to string me along like this? If he was so unhappy with me, why didn't he just divorce me and move on?

How didn't I see this coming? I was usually so aware, so astute. Why hadn't I seen the red flags or the warning signs earlier? I felt the shame enveloping me like an unwelcome foe. Blinking through the blur of my tortured tears, my gaze drifted to the nightstand where Shaun's Bible rested, like a silent witness to the chaos that had just ensued. Where was God in all of this mess? So much for going to church together.

Hypocrite, I thought. Though I wasn't sure if the accusation was directed toward him or me. Who was I kidding? It was probably both.

Strangely, the story of the prophet Hosea came to my mind right then. I knew the story well because, at times, I felt like God was playing some sick game of chess with my life, too, as he seemed to have done with Hosea's. But I wasn't Hosea. I didn't consent to marry an unfaithful spouse, having my heart crushed over and over again. I sure as heck didn't agree for my life to be used to showcase God's unconditional love for His wayward and unfaithful people. *Or had I?*

BOUNDARIES AND FORSAKING ALL OTHERS

If you knew your future spouse would eventually be unfaithful, would you still go through with the marriage? Most of us would blurt out a loud *heck no* (and possibly something stronger) because fidelity is an expectation we bring into marriage. So why do at least 40 percent of marriages experience infidelity?[xvi] And why is infidelity happening in Christian marriages at nearly the same rate as non-Christian marriages?

In my experience, one of the greatest privileges of being an ordained pastor is officiating weddings. Weddings are sacred. They launch a relationship that is altogether different from any other. A wedding is the public proclamation of the purposeful decision when a couple announces before God and *all these witnesses*,

"I choose you." Add to that the notion of covenant, and you've got a real power play on your hands.

Some of the couples I've married choose to write their own vows, but most personally-written vows (like "I promise to hold your hand forever," or "I vow to be your best friend and baby daddy," or "I will be the wind in your sails on a stormy night") are more like emotionally-charged journal entries or love letters than binding oaths. So, I always encourage these couples to use the traditional vows as well.

I usually pause when we get to the phrase, "Forsaking all others as long as we both shall live," to allow for the weight of that promise to hang in the air. Marriage is not a game, so there should be no cheating involved.

What does it mean to forsake all others? According to the dictionary, to forsake is to abandon, renounce, or turn away from entirely. No one you've been involved with before marriage should be *kept on deck* or given the status of *best friend* after you get married. Hello boundaries. Will their feelings be hurt? Maybe. But better their feelings be hurt than for your marriage to be harmed.

The problem with most unfaithful partners isn't that they don't love their spouse; it's that they don't *respect* their spouse. Their love is not enough to draw clear boundaries with other relationships. Infidelity doesn't start with sex; it starts in the heart. Hence, Lady Wisdom warns to "guard your heart above all else, for it determines the course of your life" (Proverbs 4:23).

"Set me as a seal upon your heart, as a seal upon your arm, for love is strong as death, jealousy is fierce as the grave" (Song of Songs 8:6 ESV).

Boundaries are like guardrails for the heart. They keep everyone in their proper place. Along with boundaries, we need bonds. A bond is something that restrains or strengthens; a binding agreement; a force that cements, fuses, or holds things together. This is what it means to place your spouse as a *seal* upon your heart. Your boundaries keep other people out. Your bond holds your covenant in place (even when it feels like it's unraveling).

> Boundaries are like guardrails for the heart. They keep everyone in their proper place.

I'M NOT HOSEA

I'd have had my prophet license revoked the day God commanded me—like He did Hosea—to marry someone who would be unfaithful, only to turn my marriage into Israel's object lesson. Hosea's wife, Gomer, wasn't just unfaithful; she even had children by her other lovers. Surely God could've used another illustration, right? But He needed Hosea to experience the agony of being betrayed so that he could passionately and properly preach its full consequences to the people of Israel.

I'm reminded of an evening when I stood with a friend in her driveway, the porch light catching the tears she kept batting away as she whispered how hard things had gotten. Everything was falling apart. She told me she was going to write a book called *I'm Not Job* (see the story of Job in the Bible for context). I placed a knowing hand on her shoulder, praying for peace as she navigated the storm she couldn't seem to escape.

When I got home, it hit me. If she were going to write a book called *I'm Not Job,* I would write one called *I'm Not Hosea.*

Truth is, I wasn't Hosea. I was more like the children of Israel. So are you.

How many times have we put other people, plans, and priorities before God? How many times have we turned to something or someone outside our relationship with the Lord to meet our needs? How many times have we produced things apart from God and then asked God to bless them anyway?

And how many times has God left?

Abandoned us?

Been unfaithful to us?

Not one time.

HE IS TRULY THE ONLY FAITHFUL ONE.

This is what the apostle Paul was speaking of when he wrote, "If we are unfaithful, he remains faithful, for he cannot deny who He is" (2 Timothy 2:13). Faithfulness is God's nature. He cannot deny Himself who He is. He is always true.

I'm not glossing over the ache that betrayal leaves behind. If your spouse has been unfaithful, you've felt its sting in places words barely reach. Trust me, I know it hurts. God empathizes and sympathizes with us in our pain because He's been there, too.

I share many resources on my website at danache.com, including my flagship program *Infidelity Intensive,* which can guide your next steps if your marriage

115

has been war-torn from infidelity. Get honest. Get help. Get healed. Infidelity doesn't have to be the end of your story.

When the unfaithful spouse truly repents, and the wounded spouse truly forgives, you can rebuild a whole new marriage that is more resilient and intimate than ever. This doesn't happen in every marriage, of course, but it is indeed possible. It's how my own marriage and the marriages of many couples I've coached have been healed.

The story of Hosea and Gomer illustrates God's steadfast love and forgiveness even in the face of our unfaithfulness. He is a covenant-keeping God. Hosea's willingness to marry Gomer, despite her repeated failings, mirrors God's relentless love for His people. Love is an action verb—a choice, not just a feeling. This story shows that commitment requires courage, and that even broken marriages can experience redemption and restoration when both spouses are committed to the process of repentance and forgiveness.

> Allow God to fix what's been broken, even if that just means he fixes you.

Just as God used Hosea's sacrificial love toward Gomer to illustrate His own redemptive heart, we learn that persistent, patient, and purposeful love can heal deep wounds and reveal divine worth. If you're reeling from what infidelity has stolen from you, take heart. Allow God to fix what's been broken, even if that just means He fixes you.

"Let those who are wise understand these things. Let those with discernment listen carefully. The paths of the LORD are true and right, and righteous people live by walking in them. But in those paths sinners stumble and fall" (Hosea 14:9).

APPLICATION

Wholeness and restoration, while not guaranteed, are possible after betrayal. The long process requires both spouses to choose to extend or receive mercy, forsaking the entire affair while also setting healthy, protective boundaries, being honest, and committing to rebuilding trust step by step for as long as it takes. Seek God together for healing, along with the help of a skilled marriage professional for guidance. In time, you can recreate moments of connection that reinforce loyalty and love.

Also, know that forgiveness and reconciliation are not the same. If the unfaithful spouse chooses to continue in the adulterous relationship or will not repent, reconciliation is not possible. God will not usurp human will. However, for the willing and repentant, just as God's steadfast love redeemed Gomer, you, too, can experience God's transformative restoration in your life.

CONVERSATION STARTERS

1. What boundaries can we put in place to protect our marriage from infidelity?
2. If you were betrayed in a previous relationship, have you healed? How did you do it?
3. How can we invite God into the broken places of our marriage?
4. Do you feel respected in our marriage? Why or why not?

5. Are there any unmet needs or unspoken expectations you have that could endanger our marriage?

REFLECTION

What does Hosea's relentless love for Gomer reveal to us about God's own unwavering love and pursuit of us, even when we've been unfaithful to Him?

PRAYER REQUESTS

_____

_____

_____

_____

_____

_____

PRAYER

Heavenly Father, you are faithful. You keep your promises even when we are faithless. You know everything about us. You know our deepest hurts and our darkest sins. You know us and yet you still love us. Teach us how to love one another as you love us. Where there has been betrayal in our marriage, heal, forgive, and guide us to the help we need. Allow us to be a safe place for friends or family members experiencing infidelity. Let our marriage be a testimony to your redemptive power at work in the lives of two imperfect people. In Jesus's name, Amen.

PART 4

Loyalty and Leadership

10

Mary and Joseph: A Godly Covering and Blended Families

Protecting Your Spouse from What Looks Like the Worst

This is how Jesus the Messiah was born. His mother, Mary, was engaged to be married to Joseph. But before the marriage took place, while she was still a virgin, she became pregnant through the power of the Holy Spirit. Joseph, to whom she was engaged, was a righteous man and did not want to disgrace her publicly, so he decided to break the engagement quietly.

As he considered this, an angel of the Lord appeared to him in a dream. "Joseph, son of David," the angel said, "do not be afraid to take Mary as your wife. For the child within her was conceived by the Holy Spirit. And she will have a son, and you are to name him Jesus, for he will save his people from their sins."

All of this occurred to fulfill the Lord's message through his prophet:

"Look! The virgin will conceive a child!

 She will give birth to a son,
and they will call him Immanuel,
 which means 'God is with us.'"

When Joseph woke up, he did as the angel of the Lord commanded and took Mary as his wife. But he did not have sexual relations with her until her son was born. And Joseph named him Jesus.

Matthew 1:18–25

I grew up in church. Maybe you did, too.

So many of my fondest memories revolve around church dinners and Sunday morning services, where we sang hymns and listened to my pastor stutter his way through an inspiring yet convicting sermon. But my best memories are of Sunday school, where my teachers loved and disciplined us like we were their own children and poured all their biblical knowledge into our little brains, knowing we could handle it. I ate up the Word of God like the fried chicken and soggy green beans I would consume after a Sunday evening service.

When church is your childhood backdrop, the wonders of scripture can lose their edge, sounding more like folklore than the supernatural acts they are.

However, when church is your childhood backdrop, the wonders of scripture can lose their edge, sounding more like folklore than the supernatural acts they are.

Jesus was born of a virgin. Check.

The Holy Spirit impregnated Mary. Check.

Joseph married Mary, knowing she was pregnant with a child that wasn't his. Check.

Really? This entire story is a miracle—God broke through time and space to become one of *us*!

Remember, these biblical characters weren't saints. Mary and Joseph were real human beings who lived out a real-life saga that would've made the producers of *Real Housewives* raise a brow. Don't overlook how Joseph stepped in front of Mary's shame, shielding her when the world would've gladly thrown stones.

Scholars believe Mary was around fourteen or fifteen years old when the angel Gabriel appeared to her. There are no indications in scripture that Mary's lifelong dream was to be an unmarried teen mom who carried the Messiah. She was a normal teenage girl, likely devout, but normal indeed.

Imagine her sitting crisscross applesauce on the edge of her bed, blushing innocently as she read the latest love note Joseph had dropped off earlier that day. She was just about to blow out the candle that burned steadily on her nightstand when, out of nowhere, her room was filled with a bright light, and an unsightly creature appeared at the foot of her bed.

The Bible describes angels, or celestial beings, as having eyes all over their bodies and three pairs of wings, quite different from the beautiful, princess-like beings we've created in our imaginations. Perhaps that is why angels so often said, "Do not be afraid," when they appeared to people.

They also appeared in human form, which is likely why Mary didn't seem startled when the angel Gabriel appeared to her in Luke 1:28. Scripture only says that Mary was confused and disturbed by *how* the angel greeted her.

Even so, imagine pulling the covers up over your shoulders, drifting into unconsciousness, when a random man appears at the edge of your bed. He calmly tells you that the Holy Spirit will overshadow you, and you will carry a child you never asked for. Wild, right? But this is exactly what happened to Mary.

All the while, she was engaged to marry Joseph, and their hearts—and their families—were preparing for the new life they were about to begin together. By morning, everything in her life would change.

Engagements, or betrothals, as they were called in Jewish tradition, are quite different from modern American engagements. A biblical betrothal typically lasted about a year and was contractually binding. It was an unconsummated marriage—a legally recognized agreement between a man and a woman that required a formal divorce to dissolve.[xvii] Couples could not simply call off the engagement. One would have to initiate a legal petition to void the agreement and could suffer a steep financial penalty for doing so.[xviii]

Not only that, but if a man broke off a betrothal to a woman, she would be ostracized, or worse. Everyone would assume she'd done something shameful or terrible, like adultery. If the woman was found to have been unfaithful at any time during the betrothal period or marriage, the penalty was sudden death by stoning (see Deuteronomy 22:20–21).

Remember, Mary and Joseph were *real* people.

What man would believe his fiancée if she told him that, although they had never been sexually intimate, she was somehow pregnant—but not to worry, for the child was the Holy Ghost's?

Joseph was in a real pickle here. He loved Mary, no doubt. And he likely knew she was a woman of noble character. He wouldn't have chosen her for a wife if that weren't true. But what about this baby? He knew it wasn't his. He doubted it was the Holy Spirit's either. What would everyone think of him? Of Mary?

A GODLY COVERING

We tend to associate cover-ups with blind loyalty or a *snitches-get-stitches* way of thinking. Yet some cover-ups serve a good and necessary purpose.

I imagine Joseph endured many sleepless nights as images of Mary in another man's arms haunted his thoughts. Understandably, he contemplated a public divorce. However, he didn't want to shame Mary, even if she had shamed him (Matthew 1:19).

So, he devised a plan to "put her away quietly." What might that have looked like? Perhaps he would concoct a story about how they mutually agreed that the timing just wasn't right for them to get married. Perhaps he'd say Mary was allergic to sawdust—Joseph was a carpenter, after all— and she decided she didn't want to have to take an antihistamine for the rest of her life.

What we do know is that, during Joseph's inner turmoil, an angel of God appeared to him in a dream. The angel quieted his fears, assuring him that the child Mary carried, conceived by inconceivable means, was indeed legitimate. The angel further commanded Joseph to go through with the marriage, for the baby was indeed the Messiah, the Savior of the world.

I'm sure there's a special place in heaven for Joseph because of how he covered Mary. The courage, compassion, and commitment he showed to her—and to Jesus—by stepping in as His earthly father and raising Him as his own son serve as a beautiful blueprint for every stepparent.

BLENDED FAMILIES

Recent statistics show that 40 percent of married couples raising children include stepchildren.[xix] In other words, blended families affect nearly *half* of all families with children. As divorce rates continue to rise, the number of blended families will also increase. Unfortunately, "despite the prevalence of stepfamilies and the blended family divorce rate, stepfamilies remain one of the most neglected groups in churches today," says Ron L. Deal, LMFT, LPC.[xx]

If your family includes children who are not biologically yours, you likely feel this tension. Do you ever feel excluded from parenting conversations? Or long for the Church to be more proactive in helping families navigate the turbulent waters of blended families?

My mom remarried when I was three years old. I remember wanting a dad desperately. I had only one memory of my biological father, and that was the tassels on his dress shoes. Apparently, I must have been crawling around the floor when he was nearby. However, when my stepfather came into my life, my newfound bliss was short-lived. Instead of covering my mother, my sisters, and me, he often exposed us to anger, control, and chronic episodes of domestic violence and other traumas. Sadly, my mother frequently chose to *cover* his flaws in the name of love. Friend, there is a difference between covering and enabling.

Stepparents walk a delicate line. They are called to both connect and correct. Covering your spouse and stepchildren does not equal silence or passivity. Rather, it is an ongoing dance of timing, tone, and trust. Respect is earned through faithfulness, not force. Courageous love tells the truth, but it does so in a way that protects the bond you are trying to build.

Joseph modeled wise stepparenting through his faithful presence, protective courage, and quiet obedience. In covering Mary, he gave Jesus legal lineage, social belonging, and safety. He provided materially, raising Jesus in the ordinary rhythms of work and worship.

Scripture does not record any spoken words from Joseph, but his walk was louder than his talk. His actions showed that he understood his assignment: he brought Jesus to the temple, taught him how to work, and modeled hearing the voice of the Lord. Joseph never competed with Jesus's heavenly Father, nor did he shrink from his responsibilities because "Jesus already has a dad." Instead, he embraced the role God entrusted to him, showcasing a love that shields, serves, and shows up consistently. Joseph remained faithful, even as whispers followed him and despite the quiet questions and unspoken judgments surrounding his family.

COVERING VS. ENABLING

Like Joseph, there will be times in your marriage when you choose to cover your spouse's flaws. Let's say your spouse makes a terrible financial decision that brings disgrace or shame on your family. Instead of joining the finger-pointers, you can help your spouse develop a plan to recover the lost finances and move on. Maybe your spouse's past failures ricochet years later, and you are tempted to walk away from the marriage, but then you realize God's mercy covers those past mistakes.

As I bore witness to my mother and stepfather's highly dysfunctional marriage, I found myself normalizing nonsense. I would be in my twenties before I learned about the toxic traits of codependency and enabling. They are damaging and devastating to every relationship. This is why you can't afford to cushion your spouse's character flaws, bad behavior, or abuse. Each of us must learn to take responsibility for our actions and the pain we have caused others. Owning your mistakes is a sign of emotional and spiritual maturity.

The American Psychological Association describes an enabler as "one who allows or contributes to the continued maladaptive or pathological behavior in another person." They further describe an enabler as usually an intimate partner or close friend who "passively permits or unwittingly encourages this behavior in the other person."[xxi]

Let's say your spouse can't seem to put the bottle down, even while insisting he's in complete control. If you purchase alcohol for him, for any reason, you are acting as an enabler. If your wife's credit cards are all stretched to

> Sin does not just go away. It must be confronted.

their limits, the result of impulse buys and a lifestyle her paycheck can't keep up with, yet you open a new line of credit in her name, you are acting as an enabler. If your husband is repeatedly unfaithful to you, and your solution to fix your marriage is simply to stay and pray, you are acting as an enabler.

Sin doesn't just go away. It must be confronted. Enabling is not love or even compassion; it's a pathway to codependency and continued dysfunction.

Covering your spouse's sin should only happen after genuine repentance has taken place. 1 Peter 4:8 says, "Most important of all, continue to show deep love for each other, for love covers a multitude of sins." It is crucial to understand the context of this verse. Peter was talking about the Christian's responsibility to live righteously before a watching world. Verses one through three implied that they had already finished living a life of sin, chasing after their own desires, and "taking part in the things godless people do." 1 Peter 4:8 is *not* a license to overlook the present and persistent sins of the people we love.

This doesn't mean you never extend mercy to your spouse when they sin. Just as God shows us mercy, we, too, should extend mercy to all (see Luke 6:36, James 2:13, and Matthew 5:7).

But mercy is not enabling.

Mercy recognizes sin, while enabling pretends there is no sin. Mercy doesn't say, "It's okay." Mercy loosens the grip of judgment, dialing down the consequences, while praying the restraint sparks repentance. Ask God for discernment to know when consequences should do the teaching and when you're supposed to cover your spouse while pointing them toward Jesus—their highest calling.

THE ULTIMATE COVERING

Jesus sacrificed His life for you and me. I wonder if, while He hung on the cross, He thought of how His earthly father, Joseph, covered Him and His mother. Could it be that Joseph's obedience paved the way for Jesus to cover you and me? Jesus took on Himself our shame and our sin, saving us from a sure and sudden death, and worse, eternity separated from Him. I suspect Joseph had no idea that his courageous faith and compassionate mercy would trigger a chain reaction that would reverberate for eternity.

This is the essence of *chesed* (or *hesed*), faithful, merciful, covenantal love. The word is so rich that entire books have been written about it. We may never fully understand the gravity of this word, but we get to experience it with every act of boundless mercy the Father pours on us. Might we learn to do the same for our spouses. "The faithful love of the LORD never ends! His mercies never cease" (Lamentations 3:22).

APPLICATION

When spouses make mistakes or when situations could easily invite shame, you can choose to shield them instead of shaming them. Practically, this involves refraining from airing all your spouse's faults to friends or family. It also means speaking well of them in public, even when things may be tense in private. And it includes creating a safe environment where mistakes can be acknowledged, repented for, and forgiven without fear of humiliation, retaliation, or abandonment. By protecting one another in this way, you build deeper trust and reflect Christ's love, which always seeks to restore rather than condemn.

CONVERSATION STARTERS

1. When have you felt most protected by me in our marriage? Have there been times when I've made you feel exposed or unprotected? How can I make that right?
2. What does it look like for me to cover you when you're struggling or vulnerable?
3. How can we work to provide a safer space for blended families, perhaps our own?
4. What's one way I can encourage you to be more honest and share your weaknesses or mistakes?
5. How do you think God calls us to protect each other's dignity in our marriage, especially in the presence of others?

REFLECTION

How does Joseph's choice to cover Mary rather than expose her remind you of the nature and character of God?

PRAYER REQUESTS

PRAYER

Dear Lord, thank you for the reminder that the blood of Jesus covers our sin. We are unworthy yet grateful for the kindness and mercy you've shown us. Please help us to model that same mercy to each other. Teach us how to cover each other without enabling each other. Help us to make our marriage a safe place where mistakes are forgiven and mercy is given. Protect us and our marriage from irresponsible behavior that would bring shame on our marriage and on your name. In Jesus's name we pray, Amen.

11

Ananias and Sapphira:
A Spouse Who Leads You Astray

Choosing Truth and Faithfulness Over Blind Loyalty

But there was a certain man named Ananias who, with his wife, Sapphira, sold some property. He brought part of the money to the apostles, claiming it was the full amount. With his wife's consent, he kept the rest. Then Peter said, "Ananias, why have you let Satan fill your heart? You lied to the Holy Spirit, and you kept some of the money for yourself. The property was yours to sell or not sell, as you wished. And after selling it, the money was also yours to give away. How could you do a thing like this? You weren't lying to us but to God!"

As soon as Ananias heard these words, he fell to the floor and died. Everyone who heard about it was terrified. Then some young men got up, wrapped him in a sheet, and took him out and buried him. About three hours later his wife came in, not knowing what had happened. Peter asked her, "Was this the price you and your husband received for your land?"

"Yes," she replied, "that was the price." And Peter said, "How could the two of you even think of conspiring to test the Spirit of the Lord like this? The young men who buried your husband are just outside the door, and they will carry you out, too."

Instantly, she fell to the floor and died. When the young men came in and saw that she was dead, they carried her out and buried her beside her husband. Great fear gripped the entire church and everyone else who heard what had happened

Acts 5:1–11

Let's be clear: I am not the hide-the-body type of friend.

I love my friends, God knows I do, but I ain't going to jail for nobody! Not even Shaun. I recently came across a post on social media that went like this:

Husband: If I killed someone, would you tell on me?

Wife: No, but I'd use it against you all the time. I'd be like, are you gonna walk the dog ... or do I have to make a phone call?

Ah, a woman after my own heart!

I first learned about the story of Ananias and Sapphira in my church's elementary Sunday school class. I knew nothing about marriage at that age, of course. But still, I thought Sapphira could've done better. I wondered why she didn't try to talk some sense into her husband when he concocted his devious plan. Why even lie about how much they sold their property for? The Bible clearly states that Ananias had options regarding the sale of his property. He didn't have to sell it in the first place. And why would Sapphira lie for her husband, in the house of God, of all places?

Couldn't be me ... (I was a wise child).

I knew as a pre-pubescent pupil what many women don't realize today. Submission has limitations.

> Your devotion to your spouse should never supersede your devotion to your Lord.

We must always remember that we are first believers and spouses second. Your devotion to your spouse should never supersede your devotion to your Lord.

At this critical juncture in the early Church's history, generosity had reached its peak.

> All the believers were unified in heart and mind. And they felt that what they owned was not their own, so they shared everything they had.
>
> Acts 4:32

This was the Church at her finest. There was no lack in the Church, because everyone was united and shared everything they had. Those who had more shared with those who had little. This is how it should still be, but that's another story for another day. I long for the days when the Church returns to her glory days, when we held everything in common.

DO AS I SAY, NOT AS I DO

If you want to be a terrible parent or leader, tell those under your care to "Do as I say and not as I do." This is the core of hypocrisy. The Bible clearly states that *Ananias* planned to deceive the apostles. Sapphira, however, knew full well about his plan (see Acts 5:2) and did not object. I'm sure the two of them rehearsed the story they would tell Peter and the other apostles, so their words would seem foolproof. They even likely had more lies on backup just in case Peter pressed the matter.

Remember, they didn't have to give any money if they didn't want to (see Acts 5:4). But they wanted the recognition of having done a good deed without actually doing one. They wanted to appear generous, even though they were selfish. Maybe their names would've been engraved on the stone pavement of the largest house church on the corner or boldly inscribed in the *Jerusalem Times*, who knows? Not only did they lie to man, as Peter pointed out, but they also lied to the Holy Spirit (see Acts 5:3).

God is rich in mercy, but we must be careful not to test His mercy carelessly. As Ananias's body hit the floor, he quickly learned that his lie was not worth his life. No sooner had the lie escaped his lips than God struck him dead, and his body was dragged out of the temple. Unbeknownst to Sapphira, their plan had failed. Just three hours later, she appeared before Peter, her lines rehearsed and her hands poised to receive their reward. But plot twist: as soon as she repeated the lie to Peter, God killed her, too. Dang.

STAND ON YOUR OWN TWO FEET

We've been told that united we stand, divided we fall. However, sometimes when you're united around the wrong thing, you still fall. Whether you're single or married, we are each accountable and responsible for our own conduct.

So then, each of us will give an account of ourselves to God.

Romans 14:12 NIV

When you stand before God on the great day of judgment, you will not be able to say, "My husband made me do it," or "My wife made me do it." We each have a responsibility before God to live and act righteously, regardless of what our spouse is doing or not doing.

My heart aches over how submission has been wrongly taught in many Christian denominations. Biblical submission is a requirement for *every* believer, not just women and wives (see Ephesians 5:21). Too many wives stay in abusive and unholy marriages because they think that in doing so, they are pleasing God by submitting to their husbands. But the first person we submit to is Christ. This means we base our decisions on his nature and

137

teachings. He is our highest authority, and anyone who requests or requires us to deviate from the way of Christ should be ignored. There is a godly way and a worldly way to submit. Don't confuse the two.

Collins's dictionary defines submission as "a state in which people can no longer do what they want to do because they have been brought under the control of someone else." This is worldly submission, and, sadly, it is how submission is taught in some churches. But this is not God's way. God does not want to *control* us. He wants us to exercise self-control (Galatians 5:23). He gave us free will for a purpose. And He certainly never intended for us to relinquish our free will to another fallen human being. This kind of submission may work in the armed forces, but not so much in marriage.

Submission only works when it's done willingly. God never intended for us to be subservient to one another.

Godly submission is derived from the Greek word *hupotassó*, which means a willing alignment with God-ordained order, emphasizing a dignified, voluntary response rather than coerced subservience.[xxii] Catch that. Submission only works when it's done willingly. God never intended for us to be subservient to one another. It has always been his desire that we co-labor side by side, to take dominion over the earth as equals who bear the image of God (see Genesis 1:26–28). That's why God created Eve from Adam's side, not his head to rule over him, and not his foot to be underneath him, but from his side, to lead alongside him.

When you get married, you don't leave your brain at the altar. Suppose either spouse decides to step out from under God's divine covering and starts making ungodly decisions. In that case, the other spouse has a responsibility to remain submitted to the Lord rather than to the wayward spouse. This is not my opinion. It is what the Bible teaches and models, and the story of Ananias and Sapphira illustrates this point flawlessly. Unity is a benchmark of a healthy marriage. But don't let that unity lead you astray, because united in Christ we stand, but united in sin we fall.

I find it interesting that the only people who bark submission orders to others are those who love power and lack a proper understanding of their identity in Christ.

A twenties-something couple I was coaching had major misunderstandings in their marriage. The husband, who claimed to be a Christian, though his behavior told a different story, wanted me to "teach his wife how to submit to him."

I responded decisively and directly, "How about we start with helping you learn to submit to Christ?" Needless to say, he didn't come back to coaching after that. Their dysfunction continues to this day as he wields his authority over his wife like a weapon, and she disappears into a silent shell of who God created her to be.

To be clear, I am not anti-submission … quite the contrary. I believe in a God who redeems humanity's misunderstanding and misrepresentation of His created order, and I long for my life and my marriage to reflect His original design for marriage in the garden before sin marred its image.

APPLICATION

As a couple, it's easy to fall into the trap of hiding wrongs together or presenting a false image to others in an effort to appear united. But the story of Ananias and Sapphira reminds us that unity built on deception destroys. A healthier and godlier model is to pursue unity in truth— choosing transparency over secrecy and integrity over appearances. Practically, this means being open about your struggles, pride, ungodly ambitions, and temptations, and encouraging one another toward what is right, even when it's hard or may cost you something. You can practice this by asking, "Am I helping my spouse walk in godliness, or am I enabling sin?" True oneness in marriage flourishes when both spouses are honest, accountable, and committed to prioritizing God's ways above all else.

CONVERSATION STARTERS

1. Have there been times when I encouraged you to compromise instead of calling you higher? How did that make you feel? What did you choose to do?

2. What's one area where I should hold you accountable instead of just agreeing with you?

3. Have there been moments when you felt pressured to agree with me or go along with my plan even though you disagreed? Do you think that was godly or ungodly submission? What did that feel like? What did you learn from it?

4. In light of this chapter, what are your thoughts on godly submission, and how can we practice it without enabling compromise?

5. When are we most tempted to put on a front as a couple? How can we work together to resist that?

REFLECTION

What does Acts 5 teach us about God's holiness and His desire for truth in our lives and marriage?

PRAYER REQUESTS

_____

_____

_____

_____

_____

_____

PRAYER

Father, we desire to be wholly submitted to you in all things. We want to walk in unity with each other, but help us to see when that unity threatens our submission to you. If any areas of our marriage do not align with your values, please reveal them to us. Forgive us for the times when we have sought human recognition or validation. Please help us to speak the truth, the whole truth, and nothing but the truth in love. Help us to call each other higher and not go along with any plan that is against your will. In Jesus's name, Amen.

12

Priscilla and Aquila:
Partners in Life, Love and Legacy

Leading Side by Side Without Complaining or Comparing

Then Paul left Athens and went to Corinth.
There he became acquainted with a Jew
named Aquila, born in Pontus, who had
recently arrived from Italy with his wife,
Priscilla. They had left Italy when Claudius
Caesar deported all Jews from Rome. Paul
lived and worked with them, for they were
tentmakers just as he was.

Meanwhile, a Jew named Apollos, an eloquent
speaker who knew the Scriptures well, had
arrived in Ephesus from Alexandria in Egypt.
He had been taught the way of the Lord, and
he taught others about Jesus with an
enthusiastic spirit and with accuracy.

> However, he knew only about John's baptism.
> When Priscilla and Aquila heard him preaching
> boldly in the synagogue, they took him aside
> and explained the way of God even more
> accurately

Acts 18:1–3, 24–26

Shaun and I started dating when I was fourteen, and he was seventeen. I know. I know. The age gap was a little more scandalous when we were younger than it is now. But I digress ... we were inseparable. We spent a lot of time at my neighbor's house because I often babysat her kids, and to be honest, she let us do whatever we wanted.

At the time, the youngest of her children, a two-year-old girl, would always refer to Shaun and me as *Dana and Shaun*, whether it was just me who showed up at the house or Shaun and I were together.

"Hi, Dana and Shaun!" she'd exclaim when I rang the doorbell.

"Dana and Shaun!" she'd squeal when she saw Shaun's car drive up to my house.

I held her chubby cheeks in my hands and tried to explain to her that I was just Dana, and Shaun was just Shaun. We were two different people. But it made no difference. She saw us as one. I thought it was so cute.

I get the feeling that Priscilla and Aquila had a similar kind of relationship. Their names were always mentioned together in the Bible, suggesting that the apostles and others who knew them regarded them as partners in life, work, and ministry.

Furthermore, after Paul first met Aquila, Priscilla's name is mentioned first on every occasion except for one

144

(see 1 Corinthians 16:19). This name order is significant because it likely indicates that Priscilla, the wife, carried more of the ministry weight than Aquila, the husband. Priscilla was a minister in her own right; she was not merely a minister's wife.

UNITY DONE RIGHT

In the previous chapter, you read about a couple who did unity the wrong way. Here we see unity done right. Priscilla and Aquila were first coworkers in the secular realm. They were tentmakers like Paul. They were business partners who likely shared the workload, co-led a team of apprentices, and made joint financial decisions for their business. There is no indication in Scripture that they were in ministry when Paul first met them.

We do not know when Priscilla and Aquila first began a relationship with Jesus, but it likely occurred while Paul was staying with them in their home. Acts 18 explains how Paul faithfully "preached in the synagogue, trying to convince the Jews and Greeks alike ... testifying to the Jews that Jesus was the Messiah" (vs. 4-5). At some point, after hearing Paul's teachings, Priscilla and Aquila converted from Judaism to Christianity and began traveling with Paul on his missionary journeys (vs. 18).

Now, as new believers, Priscilla and Aquila were not only business partners but also ministry partners. I can imagine how exciting this time must have been for them. The scriptures they had recently learned about came to life for them, and they witnessed the many miracles Paul performed. They weren't just new believers; they were now committed followers of Jesus.

EVERY CHRISTIAN IS A MINISTER

Not too long ago, I preached a message at my church titled *Called and Commissioned*. I emphasized that every Christian has a calling and asked all the ministers of the gospel to stand up. I attend a large church with multiple campuses and services. I preached this same message at all four campuses that weekend. At every single location, the response was the same. Only a handful of people stood at my invitation for the ministers to arise. This was *after* I had spent fifteen minutes explaining that we are *all* called to be ministers of the gospel (see 2 Corinthians 5:18–19, 1 Peter 2:5, Ephesians 4:11–12, and Matthew 28:19, to name a few). Talk about the message not hitting its target! Finally, as I stood silently waiting for the congregation to *get it*, most people began to rise to their feet. Praise God.

> As a Christian, you have been called to serve Jesus and His Church and make disciples. You are a minister of the gospel!

The word *minister* simply means to serve. It does not mean someone who has been ordained in a church, nor does it only refer to those who preach, sing, or teach the gospel. As a Christian, you are called and commissioned to serve Jesus and His Church and make disciples (see Matthew 28:18–20). Therefore, *you* are a minister of the gospel.

Priscilla and Aquila figured this out. At some point, it seems Priscilla may have taken the lead in church ministerial tasks. Perhaps Aquila devoted more time to the "tentmaking ministry" to provide income for their travels and for Paul's multifaceted ministry. Possibly, Priscilla was more of a student of the word. We don't know. But it reminds us that each spouse has unique spiritual gifts that should be nurtured and practiced. There is no indication that Priscilla and Aquila ever competed in ministry.

> There are different kinds of spiritual gifts, but the same Spirit is the source of them all. There are different kinds of service, but we serve the same Lord. God works in different ways, but it is the same God who does the work in all of us.
>
> I Corinthians 12:4–6

How healthy would our churches and marriages be if we took 1 Corinthians 12 to heart? *There is no one spiritual gift that is better than another.* Because Priscilla and Aquila worked so well together as ministry partners, they were *both* able to discern when a fellow minister needed mentoring. None other than the great Apollos himself.

> When Priscilla and Aquila heard him preaching boldly in the synagogue, *they* took him aside and explained the way of God even more accurately.
>
> Acts 18:26 (emphasis mine)

This is true unity in action. Notice Priscilla didn't tell Aquila, "Since you're a man, you go over there and help Apollos. I'll stay here and pray from a distance." No. They went *together*. Neither Priscilla nor Aquila seemed to let their gender or gifts take center stage. They saw a need and, together, sought to meet it.

There are strengths you lack that your spouse excels in. Likewise, some weaknesses may trip up your spouse that are not a problem for you. *We need each other!* The enemy comes to divide and conquer, and he starts in our own homes. If he can tempt you to see your spouse as a competitor and not a collaborator, he's on a winning streak.

This is why Shaun and I work so well together. I am gifted in writing, speaking, teaching, and preaching. Shaun is gifted in mercy, compassion, patience, and hospitality. I love the camera. He loves being behind the camera. He is always punctual, while I arrive at the airport ten minutes before boarding is complete. We couldn't be any more different! And that is just how God intended it. If we were foolish (which we are not), we would get caught up in other people's opinions about what makes a *godly male* or *female leader.* We take our cues from God, not from society or religion.

The enemy comes to divide and conquer. And he starts in our homes.

Every believer has been given at least one spiritual gift from the Holy Spirit, and many have been given more than one gift. First Corinthians 12 lists nine of these spiritual gifts. This is not an exhaustive list of all the spiritual gifts, but these nine are often grouped into three categories:

REVELATION GIFTS

- **Word of wisdom:** the ability to make wise decisions and advise others with wise counsel.
- **Word of knowledge:** the ability to understand God's will and ways and how He is working in people's lives. (This gift is similar to but different from the gift of prophecy.)
- **Discerning of spirits:** the ability to distinguish between good and evil, right and wrong, and heavenly and demonic.

POWER GIFTS

- **Faith:** the ability to trust God for extraordinary results without wavering.
- **Gift of healing:** the ability to heal people's bodies, minds, and emotions, often through prayer and laying on of hands.
- **Gift of miracles:** the ability to perform supernatural acts.

SPEAKING GIFTS

- **Speaking in tongues:** the ability to speak in an unknown language in communion with the Lord.
- **Interpretation of tongues:** the ability to understand and convey to others what was spoken in an unknown tongue.
- **Prophecy:** the ability to speak for God by declaring His will for His creation, while calling the Church to live in wholehearted worship to Him.

God gives each person the gifts He chooses for them, according to His good purposes.

Notice what the preceding and final verses state:

A spiritual gift is given to each of us *so we can help each other*. It is the one and only Spirit who distributes all these gifts. *He alone decides* which gift each person should have.

1 Corinthians 12:7, 11 (emphasis mine)

Our gifts are *meant to help each other, not hinder each other*. God—not your church, denomination, upbringing, or preferences—determines the gifts you and your spouse have been given. When you understand your spiritual gifts in relation to your spouse's, you position yourself to minister properly and purposefully without performing or pouting.

Priscilla and Aquila's legacy exemplifies godly teamwork in marriage. They model what it looks like for a couple to live on mission together, using their marriage as a platform to serve God and others. Because of their selfless commitment to the gospel, the church that met in their home, and the Church overall, remained a beacon of light and hope, sending out new ministers and teachers whom this power couple undoubtedly influenced.

Do you want this for your marriage? Do you want to leave a legacy of love and loyalty? I sure do. Couples like Priscilla and Aquila show us the way. By honoring each other and their differences, they honored God. By celebrating the way God has uniquely wired you and your spouse, you also honor God.

APPLICATION

Take a lesson from Priscilla and Aquila for your marriage. You are a minister! Read 1 Corinthians 12 together and share which spiritual gifts you have been given. Now, what spiritual gifts do you see in your spouse? Remember, your gifts are given to you by God. However, you may not be aware of your spiritual gifts. This is where your spouse can help. Ask, "How can we partner with one another in God's work?"

Practically, this could mean serving together in the same ministry area at church, mentoring younger couples, or simply aligning your goals so that your marriage reflects a shared purpose rather than two separate lives. It also means seeing your home as a place of ministry—where encouragement, hospitality, grace, and truth flow freely. By working as a team, you can deepen your intimacy and impact, showing that marriage isn't just about companionship but about advancing God's kingdom together.

CONVERSATION STARTERS

1. Why do you believe God has specifically brought us together as a couple?

2. How can our marriage better reflect God's kingdom purpose rather than just our personal goals?

3. What are some ways we can use our home to bless and serve others, like Priscilla and Aquila did?

4. Do you feel like we work as a team in our marriage? Why or why not?

5. How do you think serving God together could strengthen our bond as husband and wife?

REFLECTION

What does Priscilla and Aquila's story reveal about God's desire to use ordinary couples to accomplish extraordinary kingdom work?

PRAYER REQUESTS

_____

_____

_____

_____

_____

_____

PRAYER

Dear Lord, thank you for choosing the gifts you have given to each of us. Forgive us for any time that we complained about a gift we didn't have or competed for a gift we wanted. Help us learn how to nurture each other's gifts and work together as a team, so that your kingdom may come to earth and you may be glorified. Remind us that there is no lack in your kingdom, only abundance. We thank you in advance for the fruit that will come from our lives and ministry as we seek first your kingdom (Matthew 6:33). In Jesus's name, Amen.

Afterword

Woven throughout this book is an integral theme that—when recognized and understood—has the power to transform your entire life. It is a profound and powerful word, one I alluded to in chapter 10 when Jesus offered Himself as a covering for you and me: ***chesed*** (חֶסֶד).

I fell in love with this word years ago have been on a journey ever since to uncover the richness of its meaning. Chesed (also spelled *hesed*) is what fuels the Father's pursuit of you. It is also what should fuel your love for your spouse.

Though this word cannot be reduced to a few English phrases, it is often described as covenantal and steadfast love, lovingkindness, and covenant faithfulness.[xxiii] Chesed is the kind of love that chooses forgiveness over failure, reconciliation over regret, and hope over hindrances.

Whether you realized it or not, as you've read these pages, you have encountered the God of chesed. His lovingkindness led you to pick up this book, and my prayer is that your life —and your marriage— will be forever marked by His compassionate grace.

By reading, and more importantly, applying this book in your life, you have just sown immeasurable seeds into your marriage—fertile soil for God to produce an outrageous harvest of love, joy, and peace.

The Bible frequently uses metaphors of seed, planting, and harvest. A godly couple is the foundation of a godly marriage. A godly marriage is the foundation of a godly family. Godly families are the foundation of a godly society. And a godly society reflects the kingdom of God on earth as it is in heaven (Matthew 6:10).

As you've read, my life is an open book. My marriage, like yours, is still being refined by the hand of the Lord, and He often uses trials to do just that, not because he wants you to experience the agony of pain, but because pain is often the pathway to purpose. Stay in the Master's hand.

Some people say the grass is greener on the other side, but I believe the grass is greener where it is watered. Thank you for entrusting me with guiding you through green pastures. I pray this won't be the last time you read through this book. Make it a part of your marriage rhythm. Create your own conversation starters. Put a check mark next to the prayer requests when God answers. And whatever you do, keep on praying!

Above all, never stop investing in your marriage, both spiritually and naturally.

May the chesed of the Lord lead you, shaping not only what you believe, but how you love—day by day, choice by choice.

The best is yet to come for you, my friend!

Faithfully,

About the Author

 Dana Che is a gifted communicator, marriage coach, and teaching pastor at New Life Church in Virginia Beach, VA. She joyfully and truthfully inspires others to rediscover their God-given connection. She also hosts the *Rebuilding Us* podcast, where her graceful honesty and humor shine. She holds a BA in Communication Studies from Regent University. Dana published her debut novel, *The Choice that Changed Her Life*, in 2014. No, you've never heard of it.

Dana has been married to her childhood sweetheart, Shaun, since the 1990s—the year before Y2K. They have three young adult children and one teenager. Dana's love languages are laughter and acts of vacation, and she's happiest tucked somewhere warm and cozy with her favorite people or while reading a great book. Learn more about her writing and relationship resources and follow her speaking schedule:

DanaChe.com. Click the *Speaking* page to inquire about booking Dana to speak at your event.

Follow on Social
Facebook: @MrsDanaChe
Instagram: @MrsDanaChe

DANA CHE
L E G A C Y   C O .

YOUR NEXT STEPS

Dana Che is the founder of Dana Che Legacy Co., a faith-based education, coaching, and media company, located in Virginia Beach, Virginia.

Your marriage is a story that God is still writing, and you don't have to turn the next page alone. If *Tried and True* has stirred hope, healing, or a fresh desire to grow in your faith or marriage, here are meaningful ways to keep the momentum going.

INFIDELITY INTENSIVE

If your relationship is healing from betrayal or carrying the weight of broken trust, *Infidelity Intensive* offers a guided, grace-filled path forward. Go from triage to transformation—whether healing apart or together. Learn more at DanaChe.com/InfidelityIntensive.

COVENANT CONNECTIONS

For couples who want deeper community and accountability, *Covenant Connections* provides a space where you can grow alongside others committed to a Christ-centered marriage. Through intentional  conversations, support, and tried-and-tested tools, you'll strengthen your connection and your covenant. Learn more at DanaChe.com/CovenantConnections.

REBUILDING US PODCAST

Continue your journey with weekly encouragement on the *Rebuilding Us* podcast. With over one million downloads, each episode shares real stories, biblical wisdom, and honest conversations that help you grow in connection, courage, and  clarity—no matter what chapter your marriage is in. Subscribe and listen at DanaChe.com/Podcast.

FIVE CONVERSATIONS FOR WHEN YOUR MARRIAGE IS BEING TRIED

A FREE 5-day devotional companion for couples who want to go deeper together

Five days. Five biblical reflections. Five intentional conversations—designed to help you reconnect without pressure or performance.

If this book has stirred something in you—questions, conviction, or a longing for a deeper connection—grab your FREE companion resource today.

The *Tried and True 5-Day Companion Guide* is a guided reset for your marriage and includes:

- Five short daily devotional readings

- One focused conversation starter

- Scripture-based prayer prompts

- Designed for ten to fifteen minutes a day together

Download this resource for FREE today at DanaChe.com/TriedandTrue.

Thank you so much for reading.
If you enjoyed this book, I'd really appreciate it
if you left a review on Amazon.

Your words help other couples find the hope, healing,
and encouragement they need as well.

Thank you!

Notes

Chapter 1

[i] Brené Brown, Daring Greatly: How the Courage to Be Vulnerable Transforms the Way We Live, Love, Parent, and Lead (Avery, 2015).

Chapter 4

[ii] Bible Hub, "Strong's Greek: 772. ἀσθενής (asthenés) — Weak, feeble, infirm," accessed December 2, 2025, https://biblehub.com/greek/772.htm.

[iii] Bible Hub, "Genesis 29:35 — BibleHub Commentary," accessed December 2, 2025, https://biblehub.com/genesis/29-35.htm.

Chapter 5

[iv] BibleProject, "Book of Judges," accessed December 2, 2025, https://bibleproject.com/guides/book-of-judges/.

[v] "But all things should be done decently and in order" (1 Cor. 14:40 ESV).

[vi] Jim Davis, "Where to Find the Real Proverbs 31 Woman," The Gospel Coalition, July 5, 2022, https://www.thegospelcoalition.org/article/find-proverbs-woman/.

Chapter 6

[vii] N.T., "Is There a Tradition That Song of Songs Shouldn't Be Read Until After Marriage?" Mi Yodeya (Stack Exchange), March 23, 2025, https://judaism.stackexchange.com/questions/148388/is-there-a-tradition-that-song-of-songs-shouldnt-be-read-until-after-marriage.

[viii] Rachel Scheinerman, "Why Jews Read the Song of Songs on Passover," *My Jewish Learning,* 2025, https://www.myjewishlearning.com/article/why-jews-read-the-song-of-songs-on-passover/.

[ix] Nicole K. McNichols, "What It Actually Means to Be in a Sexless Marriage," *Psychology Today,* July 14, 2025, https://www.psychologytoday.com/us/blog/everyone-on-

top/202506/are-you-in-a-sexless-marriage-heres-what-that-actually-means.

x Saul McLeod, "Maslow's Hierarchy of Needs," Simply Psychology, accessed December 2, 2025, https://www.simplypsychology.org/maslow.html.

Chapter 7

xi The Gottman Institute, "The Four Horsemen: Recognizing Criticism, Contempt, Defensiveness, and Stonewalling," Gottman Institute Blog, October 15, 2024, https://www.gottman.com/blog/the-four-horsemen-recognizing-criticism-contempt-defensiveness-and-stonewalling/.

xii Bible Hub, "Strong's Hebrew: 6406. פַּלְטִי (Palti)—Palti," accessed December 2, 2025, https://biblehub.com/hebrew/6406.htm.

xiii John L. Kachelman Jr., "Michal: A Character Study," Christian Library, accessed December 2, 2025, https://www.christianlibrary.org/authors/John_L_Kachelman_Jr/people-ot/michal.htm.

xiv The Gottman Institute, "The Four Horsemen: Recognizing Criticism, Contempt, Defensiveness, and Stonewalling," Gottman Institute Blog, October 15, 2024, https://www.gottman.com/blog/the-four-horsemen-recognizing-criticism-contempt-defensiveness-and-stonewalling/.

xv The Gottman Institute, "The Four Horsemen."

Chapter 9

xvi Scott D. Haltzman, The Secrets of Surviving Infidelity (Baltimore: Johns Hopkins University Press, 2013).

Chapter 10

xvii Marcus Jastrow and Bernard Drachman, "Betrothal," in The Jewish Encyclopedia, ed. Isidore Singer, vol. 3 (Funk & Wagnalls, 1903), 125–28.

xviii Jastrow and Drachman, "Betrothal," 125.

xix Consuegra, Claudio, and Pamela Consuegra, eds. Journal of Family Research and Practice: Blended Families. Vol. 2, no. 1. North American Division of the Seventh-day Adventist Church, 2022.

[xx] Consuegra and Consuegra, Journal of Family Research and Practice.

[xxi] "Enabling," *APA Dictionary of Psychology* (American Psychological Association, n.d.), accessed December 02, 2025, https://dictionary.apa.org/enabling

Chapter 11

[xxii] Bible Hub, "Strong's Greek: 5292. ὑποταγή (hupotagé)—Submission, subjection," accessed December 2, 2025, https://biblehub.com/greek/5292.htm

Afterword

[xxiii] Card, Michael. Inexpressible: Hesed and the Mystery of God's Lovingkindness. Downers Grove, IL: InterVarsity Press, 2018.